BERLITZ®

ARABIC
FOR TRAVELLERS

By the staff of Editions Berlitz

Library of Congress Catalog Card Number: 74-1978

13th printing 1985

Printed in Hungary

Editions Berlitz
1, avenue des Jordils
1000 Lausanne 6, Switzerland

Preface

You are about to visit an Arabic-speaking country. Our aim is to give you a practical phrase book to help you on your trip. *Arabic for travellers* provides:

* all the phrases and supplementary vocabulary you will need on your trip
* a wide variety of tourist and travel facts, tips and useful information
* a complete phonetic transcription, showing you the pronunciation of all the words and phrases listed
* special sections showing the replies your listener might give to you—just hand him the book and let him point to the appropriate phrase. This is especially practical in certain difficult situations (doctor, car mechanic, etc.). It makes direct, quick and sure communication possible
* a logical system of presentation so that you can find the right phrase for the immediate situation
* quick reference through colour coding. The major features of the contents are on the back cover; a complete index is given inside.

These are just a few of the practical advantages. In addition, the book will prove a valuable introduction to life in the Arab world.

There is a comprehensive section on Eating Out, giving translations and explanations for pratically anything one might find on a menu in the Middle East; there is a complete Shopping Guide that will enable you to obtain virtually anything you want. Trouble with the car? Turn to the mechanic's manual with its dual-language instructions. Feeling ill? Our medical section provides the most rapid communication possible between you and the doctor.

To make the most of *Arabic for Travellers,* we suggest that you start with the "Guide to Pronunciation". Then go on to "Some Basic Expressions". This not only gives you a minimum vocabulary, it helps you to pronounce the language.

With the Arabic used in this book you can make yourself understood throughout the Middle East. Of course there are considerable differences in vocabulary and usage (see next page). That's why you will sometimes find alternatives for words given in brackets [ ]. If your listener cannot understand the first expression, try the alternative.

We are particularly grateful to Mr. Aly Hussein, Dr. Z. Mahfouz of the Berlitz Schools of Egypt, Mr. Habib Rahme and Mr. Shukri Taher for their help in the preparation of this book, and also to Dr. T.J.A. Bennett for his advice concerning the transliteration. We also wish to thank Egyptair for its assistance.

We shall be very pleased to receive any comments, criticisms and suggestions that you think may help us in preparing future editions. Thank you. Have a good trip.

Throughout this book, the symbols illustrated here indicate small sections where phrases have been compiled that your foreign listener might like to say to **you.** If you don't understand him, give him the book and let him point to the phrase in his language. The English translation is just beside it.

A very basic grammar

Classical Arabic is the language of the Koran and dates back to the 7th century. But it has changed through the centuries, and modern spoken Arabic varies greatly from country to country.

This book, destined principally for Egypt, Lebanon and Jordan—but equally useful for the rest of the Middle East—tries to steer a middle course between the spoken and the written (classical) language. When the same (spoken) word is used in all countries, we give that word as the most direct means of communication with the people. But when the word is different from one country to another, we've provided the written (classical) word which is necessarily the same in all countries. Sometimes, however, the classical word is unfamiliar and almost never used. In this case you'll find the Egyptian word with the word(s) used in other countries in brackets [ ].

Arabic is a Semitic language and therefore differs structurally from English and European concepts of language. It is written from right to left.

Articles

The definite article (the) in Arabic is ال **(æl)** for both the masculine and feminine genders, and the singular and plural. It preceeds the noun and generally the adjective.

فندق	**fon**dok	hotel
كبير	kæ**bīr**	big
الفندق	æl **fon**dok	the hotel
الفندق الكبير	æl **fon**dok æl kæ**bīr**	the big hotel

There is no indefinite article (a/an). To give indefinite meaning the article is simply omitted.

GRAMMAR

Nouns

There are two genders, masculine and feminine. In general words ending in **æ** or **a** are feminine. The names of towns and countries are nearly always feminine.

	Masculine			Feminine	
طالب	tālib	student (m.)	طالبة	tālibæ	student (f.)
شارع	shæri'	street	وردة	wærdæ	flower
دكان	dokkæn	shop	فرنسا	faransa	France

There are two sorts of plurals in Arabic: one for two things (double), and another for three or more. Basically, to form the double add the ending ين **(ēn)** to a singular masculine noun, or تين **(tēn)** to a feminine noun. To make the plural for three or more, add the ending ين **(īn)** to singular masculine nouns and ات **(æt** or **āt)** to feminine nouns. There are, however, numerous exceptions and irregular plurals where the word changes, like the English "child" to "children". Here are a few examples:

Regular

فنان	fænn**æn**	an artist	شجرة	shagara	a tree
فنانين	fænnæn**ēn**	two artists	شجرتين	shagar**tēn**	two trees
فنانين	fænnæn**īn**	artists	شجرات	shagar**āt**	trees

Irregular

ولد	wælæd	a boy	سمكة	sæmækæ	a fish
ولدين	wælæd**ēn**	two boys	سمكتين	sæmæk**tēn**	two fish
أولاد	'æwl**æ**d	boys	سمك	sæmæk	fish

Adjectives

Adjectives do not come before the noun as in English, but afterwards. They agree with the noun in gender and number. Don't forget that when there is a definite article in front of the noun, the adjective must also be preceeded by the definite article. However, the verb "to be" doesn't exist in the present tense in Arabic. In order to describe something, just put the noun with the definite article, and then the adjective without the article.

البيت الكبير	æl bēt æl kæ**bīr**	the big house
البيت كبير .	æl bēt kæ**bīr**	The house is big.

When an adjective qualifies a plural noun that is not human, the adjective is put in the feminine singular.

شجرة كبيرة	**sha**gara kæ**bī**ræ	a big tree
شجرات كبيرة	shaga**rāt** kæ**bī**ræ	big trees

There are no possessive adjectives; instead a suffix is added to the noun. Here are the suffixes for masculine nouns (for feminine nouns insert the letter **t** shown in parentheses):

my	ى . . .	...(t)i	our	نا . . .	...(t)nǣ
your(m.)	ك . . .	...(t)æk			
your(f.)	ك . . .	...(t)ik	your(pl.)	كم . . .	...(t)kom
his/its	ه . . .	...(t)oh			
her/its	ها . . .	...(t)hæ	their	هم . . .	...(t)hom

Adding a possessive pronoun suffix to a noun makes it definite, and therefore if an adjective follows, the adjective must have the definite article.

كتاب كبير	ki**tǣb** kæ**bīr**	a big book
كتابى الكبير	ki**tǣ**bi æl kæ**bīr**	my big book

Verbs

One particularity of Arabic verbs is that they change not only according to the subject (I, you, he, etc.), but also according to whether a man or a woman is spoken to. You'll find examples of this in "Some Basic Expressions" (pages 16–21). In the rest of this phrase book all verbs are given in the masculine form, unless the context shows clearly that you're addressing a woman.

The following is the past and present conjugation of the verb "to write". Note that the subject pronoun is normally omitted.

	Present tense		Past tense	
I	أكتب	'æktob	كتبت	kætæbto
you (m.)	تكتب	tæktob	كتبت	kætæbtæ
you (f.)	تكتبى	tæktobi	كتبتى	kætæbti
he/it	يكتب	yæktob	كتب	kætæbæ
she/it	تكتب	tæktob	كتبت	kætæbæt
we	نكتب	næktob	كتبنا	kætæbnǣ
you	تكتبوا	tæktobū	كتبتوا	kætæbtū
they	يكتبوا	yæktobū	كتبوا	kætæbū

To form the future tense, add the prefix سا (sæ) to the present tense.

When you want to make a negative sentence, put ما (mǣ) in front of the verb:

أنا أكتب .	ænǣ 'æktob	I write.
أنا ما أكتب .	ænǣ mǣ 'æktob	I don't write.

To ask a question, simply put هل (hæl) at the beginning of the sentence:

البيت كبير .	æl bēt kæbīr	The house is big.
هل البيت كبير ؟	hæl æl bēt kæbīr	Is the house big?

Personal pronouns

I	أنا	ænǣ	we	نحن	næḥno
you (m.)	أنت	'intæ			
you (f.)	انت	'inti	you	أنتم	'æntom
he/it	هو	howæ			
she/it	هى	hiyæ	they	هم	hom

GRAMMAR

Guide to pronunciation

Here are the 28 characters which comprise the Arabic alphabet. A character may have different forms, depending on whether it's used by itself or comes at the end, in the middle or at the beginning of a word.

Isolated	Final	Median	Initial	Name
ا	ـا			'ælif
ب	ـب	ـبـ	بـ	bi
ت	ـت	ـتـ	تـ	ti
ث	ـث	ـثـ	ثـ	si
ج	ـج	ـجـ	جـ	gim
ح	ـح	ـحـ	حـ	ḥa
خ	ـخ	ـخـ	خـ	kha
د	ـد			dæl
ذ	ـذ			zæl
ر	ـر			ri
ز	ـز			zēn
س	ـس	ـسـ	سـ	sīn
ش	ـش	ـشـ	شـ	shin
ص	ـص	ـصـ	صـ	sād
ض	ـض	ـضـ	ضـ	da
ط	ـط	ـطـ	طـ	ta
ظ	ـظ	ـظـ	ظـ	za
ع	ـع	ـعـ	عـ	'ēn
غ	ـغ	ـغـ	غـ	g̣ēn
ف	ـف	ـفـ	فـ	fi
ق	ـق	ـقـ	قـ	kāf
ك	ـك	ـكـ	كـ	kæf
ل	ـل	ـلـ	لـ	læm
م	ـم	ـمـ	مـ	mīm
ن	ـن	ـنـ	نـ	nūn
ه ة	ـة ـه	ـهـ	هـ	hi
و	ـو			wāw
ى	ـى	ـيـ	يـ	yi

This, of course, is not enough to pronounce Arabic. We're offering you a helping hand by providing a transcription throughout this book. This and the following section are intended to make you familiar with our transcription and to help you get used to the sounds of Arabic.

As a minimum vocabulary for your trip, we've selected a number of basic words and phrases under the title "Some Basic Expressions" (pages 16–21).

An outline of the sounds of Arabic

The traditional Arabic script is composed of consonants only and is written from right to left. A system of vowel signs (small marks above or below the characters), used mainly in the Koran, in poetry and in texts for beginners ensures proper pronunciation.

Written Arabic is fairly uniform. The spoken language, however, can differ considerably from one country to another or even among regions of the same country. We have based our transcription on the dialect used in most parts of Lower Egypt and especially in Cairo. This dialect is widely understood throughout the Middle East thanks to Egyptian films, radio and the recordings of popular artists. In addition, the Egyptian dialect is easier to learn than the others because some difficult sounds have been replaced by simpler ones, so that several letters of the alphabet are pronounced alike.

You'll find the pronunciation of the Arabic letters and sounds explained below, as well as the symbols we use for them in the transcriptions. Of course, the sounds of any two languages are never exactly the same; but if you follow carefully the indications supplied here, you'll have no difficulty in reading our transcriptions in such a way as to make yourself understood.

Letters written **bold** should be stressed (pronounced louder).

Consonants

Letter	Approximate pronunciation	Symbol	Example
ء أ	glottal stop*	ʼ	أرنب ʼ**æ**rnæb
ب	like **b** in **b**oy	b	باب b**ǣ**b
ت	like **t** in **t**en	t	تاج t**ǣ**g
ث	in classical Arabic, like **th** in **th**in; in spoken Arabic:		
	1) like **s** in **s**it	s	ثورة s**a**wra
	2) like **t** in **t**en	t	ثور t**ō**r
ج	1) like **g** in **g**et (Egypt)	g	جميل gæm**ī**l
	2) like **s** in plea**s**ure (most other countries)	zh	جميل zhæm**ī**l
ح	like **h** in **h**oot, but more "emphatic" and with slight friction in throat	ḥ	حديد ḥæd**ī**d
خ	like **ch** in Scottish lo**ch**	kh	خرج **kh**aragæ
د	like **d** in **d**ay	d	دب d**i**bb
ذ	in classical Arabic, like **th** in **th**en; in spoken Arabic:		
	1) like **z** in **z**ebra	z	ذكى z**æ**ki
	2) like **d** in **d**ay	d	ذهب d**æ**hæb
ر	like **r** in rolled Scottish **r**	r	رجل r**ā**gil

* This corresponds, in English, to the initial blocking of the throat before a vowel, as before the second o in "cooperate". It is also heard in the Cockney pronunciation of t in "water" (wa'er). In Arabic, the glottal stop can occur before a vowel *or* a consonant and even at the end of a word.

ز	like **z** in **z**ebra	z	زيت	zēt
س	like **s** in **s**it	s	سبب	sæbæb
ش	like **sh** in **sh**ine	sh	شمس	shæms
ص	like **s** in **s**un, pronounced with considerable "emphasis"	s	صبر	sabr
ض	like **d** in **d**uck, pronounced with "emphasis"	d	ضيف	dēf
ط	like **t** in **t**ough, pronounced with "emphasis"	t	طيارة	tayyāra
ظ	in classical Arabic, like **th** in **th**en; in spoken Arabic: like **z** in **z**ebra	z	ظريف	zarīf
ع	similar to glottal stop (see above)	'	رفيع	rafī'
غ	like a soft version of **ch** in Scottish lo**ch** (or like French pronunciation of **r** in "rue")	g	غالى	gǣli
ف	like **f** in **f**eed	f	فانوس	fænūs
ق	in classical Arabic, an "emphatic" **k**; in spoken Arabic: 1) like **k** in **k**ite	k	قلب	kalb
	2) glottal stop (see above)	'	قمر	'amar
ك	like **k** in **k**ite	k	كتاب	kitǣb
ل	like **l** in **l**et	l	لطيف	latīf
م	like **m** in **m**eet	m	ملبن	mælbæn
ن	like **n** in **n**eat	n	نرجس	nærgis
ه	like **h** in **h**ear, whatever its position in the word	h	هرم	haram
و	like **w** in **w**ell	w	ورد	wærd
ى	like **y** in **y**ell	y	يكتب	yæktob

Vowels

The letters ا, و and ى in the list above can also serve as vowels. In addition, Arabic has three vowel signs (´, ʼ, ˏ); they occur either above or below the letter and are pronounced after the letter that carries the sign. In contemporary written Arabic—as in this book—the vowel signs are generally omitted. The context shows the reader which is the appropriate vowel he has to supply.

´ ا	1) like **a** in northern English h**a**t or in American wh**a**t (short)	a	صبر	sabr
	2) like **a** in car (long)	ā	طار	tār
	3) like **a** in can(short)	æ	كتب	**k**æt**æ**b**æ**
	4) like **a** in can, but long	ǣ	كتاب	kit**ǣ**b
ʼ و	1) like **aw** in ra**w**, but with the lips more tightly rounded; it sounds quite reminiscent of **oo** in f**oo**t (short)	o	بن	bonn
	2) like **ou** in f**ou**r (long)	ō	يوم	yōm
	3) like **oo** in b**oo**t (long)	ū	نور	nūr
ى	1) like **i** in s**i**t (short)	i	من	min
	2) like **ee** in m**ee**t (long)	ī	جميل	gæ**mīl**
	3) like **ay** in d**ay**, but a pure vowel, not a diphthong (long)	ē	بيت	bēt

Note

1) Each symbol in our transcriptions should be pronounced as shown above, regardless of its position in the word; e.g., **s** always has—even between two vowels or at the end of a word—to be pronounced as in sit, not as in houses.

2) Any consonants written double must be pronounced long; e.g., **kk** should be pronounced like in thi**ck c**oat, **pp** like in lam**p p**ost, **ss** like in ma**ss s**urvey, etc.

Some basic expressions

Yes.	أيوه .	æywæ
No.	لا .	læ
Please.	من فضلك . *	min fadlak*
Thank you.	شكراً .	shokran
Thank you very much.	شكراً جزيلا .	shokran gæzīlæn
That's all right.	عفواً .	æfwæn

Greetings

Good morning.	صباح الخير .	sabāḥil khēr
Good afternoon.	نهارك سعيد . **	nahārak sæīd**
Good evening.	مساء الخير .	masā'il khēr
Good night.	ليلة سعيدة .	lēlæ sæida
Good-bye.	مع السلامة .	mæ'æl sælǣmæ
See you later.	الى اللقاء .	ilæl lika'
This is Mr...	أقدم السيد . . .	okaddim assæyid
This is Mrs...	أقدم السيدة . . .	okaddim issæyidæ
This is Miss...	أقدم الآنسة . . .	okaddim il ǣnisæ

As pointed out in the grammar section, verbs in Arabic change their endings depending whether the person addressed is a man or a woman. In this section, the phrases said to a **man** are marked with one asterisk (*); those said to a **woman** are marked with two asterisks (**). Phrases not marked do not change.

I'm very pleased to meet you.	تشرّفنا .	tæsharrafna
How are you?	كيف حالك ؟ **	kæyfæ ḥǣlik**
Very well, thank you.	بخير .	bikhēr
And you?	وأنت ؟ **	wæ inti**
Fine.	كويسة . **	kwæyyisæ**
Excuse me.	آسفة .	'æsfæ

Questions

Where?	أين ؟	æynæ
Where's...?	أين . . . ؟	æynæ
Where are...?	أين . . . ؟	æynæ
When?	متى ؟	mætæ
What?	ما ؟	mæ
How?	كيف ؟	kæyfæ
How much?	كم ؟	kæm
How many?	كم ؟	kæm
Who?	من ؟	mæn
Why?	لماذا ؟	limǣzæ
Which?	أى . . . ؟	æyy
What do you call this?	ما اسم هذا ؟	mǣ ism hǣzæ
What do you call that?	ما اسم ذاك ؟	mǣ ism zǣk
What does this mean?	ما معنى هذا ؟	mæ mæ'nǣ hǣzæ
What does that mean?	ما معنى ذاك ؟	mǣ mæ'nǣ zǣk

Do you speak...?

Do you speak English?	هل تتكلم انجليزى ؟ *	hæl tætækællæm 'ingilīzi*
Do you speak German?	هل تتكلمى ألمانى ؟ **	hæl tætækællæmi 'almāni**
Do you speak French?	هل تتكلم فرنسى ؟ *	hæl tætækællæm firinsi*
Do you speak Spanish?	هل تتكلمى أسبانى ؟ **	hæl tætækællæmi 'æspæni**
Do you speak Italian?	هل تتكلم ايطالى ؟ *	hæ tætækællæm 'itāli*
Could you please speak more slowly?	من فضلك تكلمى على مهلك . **	min fadlik tækællæmi 'ælæ mæhlik**
Please point to the phrase in the book.	من فضلك أشر الى الجملة فى الكتاب . *	min fadlak æshir ilæl gomlæ fi æl kitæb*
Just a minute. I'll see if I can find it in this book.	لحظة واحدة . سأبحث عنها فى الكتاب .	laḥza wæḥidæ sæ'æb ḥæs 'ænhæ fi æl kitæb
I understand.	أنا أفهم .	ænæ æfhæm
I don't understand.	أنا لا أفهم .	ænæ læ æfhæm

Can...?

Can I have...?	أريد ... من فضلك ؟ *	orīd...min fadlak*
Can we have...?	نريد ... من فضلك ؟ **	norīd... min fadlik**
Can you show me...?	ممكن أن ترينى ... ؟ *	momkin æn torīni
Can you tell me...?	ممكن تقوليلى . . . ؟ **	momkin ti'ūlili**
Can you please help me?	ممكن تساعدينى من فضلك ؟ **	momkin tisæ'idīni min fadlik**

Wanting

I'd like…?	آريد ...	orīd
We'd like…?	نريد ...	norīd
Please give me…?	* من فضلك اعطنى . . . ؟	min **fad**lak a'tini*
Give it to me, please.	** . من فضلك اعطيهالى	min **fad**lik 'aatīhæ li**
Please bring me…	** ...من فضلك احضرى لى	min **fad**lik ahdiri li**
Bring it to me, please.	* . من فضلك احضرها لى	min **fad**lak iḥ**dir**hæ li*
I'm hungry.	أنا جعانة .	ænæ gæ'**ǣ**næ
I'm thirsty.	أنا عطشان .	ænæ '**at**shān
I'm tired.	أنا تعبانة .	ænæ tææ**bǣ**næ
I'm lost.	أنا تهت .	ænæ toht
It's important.	انه مهم .	innæho **mo**him
It's urgent.	انه عاجل .	innæho **ǣ**gil
Hurry up!	بسرعة !	bisor'æ

It is/There is…

It's...	انه ...	innæho
Is it...?	هل هو ... ؟	hæl **ho**wæ
It isn't...	انه ليس ...	innæho **læy**sæ
There's/There are...	يوجد ...	yūgæd
Is there/Are there...?	هل يوجد ... ؟	hæl yūgæd
There isn't/There aren't...	لا يوجد ...	lǣ yūgæd
There isn't any/There aren't any.	لا يوجد منه .	lǣ yūgæd **min**ho

A few common words

big/small	كبير / صغير	kæbir/sagir
quick/slow	سريع / بطيء	særi'/bati'
early/late	مبكر / متأخر	mobækkir/mit'akhkhar
cheap/expensive	رخيص / غالى	rakhis/gǣli
near/far	قريب / بعيد	karib/bæ'īd
hot/cold	ساخن / بارد	sǣkhin/bǣrid
full/empty	مليان / فاضى	mælyæn/fādi
easy/difficult	سهل / صعب	sæhl/sa'b
heavy/light	ثقيل / خفيف	ti'il/khæfif
open/shut	مفتوح / مقفول	mæftūh/mæ'fūl
right/wrong	صحّ / غلط	saḥḥ/galat
old/new	قديم / جديد	'ædim/gædid
old/young	عجوز / شاب	'ægūz/shæb
beautiful/ugly	جميل / وحش	gæmil/wihish
good/bad	حسن / سيء	hæsin/sæyyi'
better/worse	أحسن / أسوأ	æhsæn/æswæ'

A few prepositions and some more useful words

at	عند	'indæ
on	على	ælæ
in	فى	fi
to	الى	'ilǣ
from	من	min
inside	داخل	fiddǣkhil
outside	خارج	fi æl khǣrig
up	فوق	fō'
down	تحت	tæḥt
before	قبل	kabl
after	بعد	bæ'd

with	مع	mæ'æ
without	بدون	bidūn
through	خلال	khilǣl
towards	الى	'ilǣ
until	حتى	ḥættǣ
during	أثناء	'æsnǣ'
and	و	wǣ
or	أو	æww
not	ليس ـ غير	læysǣ gēr
nothing	لا شيء	lǣ shæy'
none	ولا واحد	wælæ wǣḥid
very	... جداً	...giddæn
also	كمان	kæmæn
soon	قريباً	karībæn
perhaps	ربما	robbæmæ
here	هنا	honæ
there	هناك	honǣk
now	الآن	æl'ǣn
then	بعدين	bæædēn

Arrival

You've arrived. Whether you've come by ship or plane, you'll have to go through passport and customs formalities. You'll doubtless have received a customs-declaration form on board. Filling it in before landing will save you time upon arrival. (For car/border control, see page 145.)

There's certain to be somebody around who speaks English. That's why we're making this a brief section.

Passport control

Your travel agent probably helped you obtain a visa and told you about vaccination requirements for the countries you intend to visit. (Failure to comply with these procedures in advance may cause you unnecessary and time-consuming complications upon arrival in the Middle East.)

Here's my passport.	هذا جواز سفرى .	hǣzæ gæwǣz safarī
I'll be staying...	سأبقى ...	sæ'abka
a few days	بضعة أيام	bid'at 'æyyǣm
a week	أسبوع	osbū
2 weeks*	أسبوعين	osbū'ēn
a month	شهر	shahr
I don't know yet.	لا أعرف بعد .	læ aarif bæ'd
I'm here on holidays.	أنا هنا فى أجازة .	ænǣ honǣ fi 'ægǣzæ
I'm here on business.	أنا هنا لشغل .	ænǣ honǣ li shogl
I'm just passing through.	أنا مارر من هنا بس .	ænǣ mǣrir min honæ bæss
I'm sorry, I don't understand. Is there anyone here who speaks English?	آسف لا أفهم . هل يوجد هنا أحد يتكلم الانجليزية ؟	ǣsif lǣ æfhæm. hæl yūgæd honæ æḥæd yætækællæm ingilīzi

* see grammar

Customs

After having your passport stamped by an immigration officer you'll go to customs. The customs officer will either have a quick look at your luggage or just ask what you have in addition to duty-exempt items. The chart below shows what you can bring in duty-free (all allowances are subject to change without notice).

	 Cigarettes		 Cigars		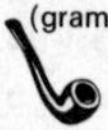 (grams) Tobacco	 Liquor (Spirits)
Egypt	400	or	50	or	250	1
Jordan	200	or	25	or	200	1*
Lebanon	500	or	25	or	200	1

* open bottle only; non Jordanians only

A customs declaration is compulsory in certain Arab countries. You must list all currency, jewellery and mechanical or electrical appliances you're bringing in (cameras, radios, etc.). One copy of this form must be given to the customs officer. You'll keep the other which will be submitted to customs upon your departure. The above items, if personal effects, are duty-free; all the governments want to prevent is their being sold or exchanged by tourists.

I've nothing to declare.	ليس عندى شيء أعلن عنه .	læysæ indi shæy' **oolin** '**æ**nho
I've...	عندى ...	indi
a carton of cigarettes	خرطوشة سجاير	khartūshit sæ**gæ**yir
a bottle of whisky	زجاجة وسكى	zo**gæ**git **wis**ki
a bottle of wine	زجاجة نبيذ	zo**gæ**git ni**bīt**
Must I pay on this?	هل يجب أن أدفع عن هذا ؟	hæl yæ**gib** æn' **æd**fæ æn **hæ**zæ

How much?	كم ؟	kæm
It's for my personal use/It's not new.	انها لاستعمالى الشخصى / انها مستعملة .	innæhæ lissti'mæli æshshakhsi/innæhæ mosta'malæ

من فضلك افتح هذه الشنطة.	Please open this bag.
يجب أن تدفع جمرك عن هذا .	You'll have to pay duty on this.
من فضلك ادفع فى المكتب الموجود هناك .	Please pay at the office over there.
هل عندك أمتعة أخرى ؟	Have you any more luggage?

Changing money

Travellers aren't allowed to bring Egyptian pounds into Egypt, so don't try to change your money before leaving. You'll have to fill in a form stating how much money you have in cash and traveller's cheques. Keep the copy of this form, for you'll have to present it when you leave, along with each receipt you receive from a bank when you change money during your stay.

You'll be able to change money at a bank at any arrival point.

I want to change some...	أريد تحويل ...	orīd tæḥwīl
traveller's cheques	شيكات سياحية	shikæt siyæḥiyyæ
dollars	دولارات	dolarāt
pounds	جنيهات	gonæyhæt
Where's the nearest bank?	أين أقرب بنك ؟	æynæ akrab bænk orīd tæḥwīl
What's the exchange rate?	ما سعر التحويل ؟	mæ si'r il tæḥwīl

Baggage—Porters

Porter!	! [عتال] شيال	shæyyæl [ættæl]
Can you help me with my luggage?	من فضلك ساعدني فى حمل الحقائب !	min fadlak sæ'idni fi ḥæml il ḥæka'ib
That's mine.	هذه لى .	hæzihi li
The big/small/blue/ brown/plaid one.	الكبيرة / الصغيرة / الزرقاء / البنى / المربعات.	æl kæbira/æl sagira/æl zærkā'/æl bonni/æl morabba'æt
There's one piece missing.	ناقص قطعة .	nākis kit'a
Take these bags to the…	خذ هذه الحقائب الى ...	khodd hæzihi il ḥakā'ib ilæ
taxi	التاكسى	æl tæksi
bus	الأوتوبيس	æl 'otobis
left-luggage office	الأمانات	æl 'æmænæt
How much is that?	بكم هذا ؟	bikæm hæzæ
Get me a taxi, please .	اطلب لى تاكسى من فضلك	otlob li tæksi min fadlak

Note: Porters' rates vary from one country to another. Have some small change ready. (For tipping, see inside back-cover.)

Directions

How do I get to…?	كيف أصل الى ... ؟	kæyfæ asil ilæ
Is there a bus into town?	هل يوجد أوتوبيس للبلد ؟	hæl yūgæd otobis lil bælæd
Where can I get a taxi?	أين أجد تاكسى ؟	æynæ 'ægid tæksi
Where can I rent a car?	أين يمكن تاجير سيارة ؟	æynæ yomkin tæ'gir sæyyāra

FOR NUMBERS, see page 175

Car rental

Car rental agencies operate in most larger centers and rates are usually attractive. You will also be able to hire chauffeur-driven cars through agencies located at most airpots as well as in major cities. It's highly likely that someone at the car-rental agency will speak English, but if nobody does, try one of the following:

I'd like to rent...	أريد تأجير ...	orīd tæ'gir
a small car	سيارة صغيرة	sæyyāra sagīra
a large car	سيارة كبيرة	sæyyāra kæbīra
a sports car	سيارة سبور	sæyyāra spōr
I'd like it...	أريدها ...	orīdohǣ
for a day/for 4 days	لمدة يوم / لمدة أربعة أيام	limoddit yōm/limoddit 4 æyyǣm
for a week/for 2 weeks	لمدة أسبوع / لمدة أسبوعين	limoddit osbū/limoddit osbu'ēn
I'd like to hire a chauffeur-driven car.	أريد تأجير سيارة بسائق [رميس] .	orīd tæ'gir sæyyāra bisǣ'ik (ramis)
What's the charge per day?	كم الثمن ليوم ؟	kæm il tæmæn liyōm
What's the charge per week?	كم الثمن لأسبوع ؟	kæm il tæmæn li 'osbū
Does that include mileage?	هل هذا يشمل العداد ؟	hæl hǣzæ yæshmæl il 'æddǣd
Does that include the services of a chauffeur?	هل هذا يشمل السائق ؟	hæl hǣzæ yæshmæl il sǣ'ik
Is petrol (gasoline) included?	هل هذا يشمل البنزين ؟	hæl hǣzæ yæshmæl il bænzin
Does that include full insurance?	هل هذا يشمل التأمين الشامل ؟	hæl hǣzæ yæshmæl il tæ'mīn il shǣmil
What's the deposit?	كم التأمين ؟	kæm il tæ'min
I have a credit card.	عندى بطاقة رصيد مصرفى .	indi bitākit rasīd masrafī

* see grammar

FOR DRIVING LICENCE, see page 145

Taxi

All taxis have meters, but you might ask the approximate fare beforehand.

In addition to taxis, you'll find a collective-taxi service (sær**vis**) in Lebanon. This is a type of group taxi which follows a fixed route, picking up and letting passengers off along the way. Each pays the same fare and can get on or off anywhere he wishes along the route. This is a very popular means of transportation within cities as well as for inter-urban trips. Collective taxis are cheap, costing scarcely more than the bus.

Where can I get a taxi?	أين أجد تاكسى ؟	æ**y**næ ægid **tæ**ksi
Get me a taxi, please.	أطلب لى تاكسى من فضلك .	**ot**lob li **tæ**ksi min **fad**lak
What's the fare to...?	كم الثمن الى ... ؟	kæm il**tæ**mæn **ilæ**
How far is it to...?	ما المسافة الى ... ؟	mæ æl mæ**sæ**fæ **ilæ**
Take me to...	خذنى الى ...	**khod**ni ilæ
this address/the town centre/the ... hotel	هذا العنوان/ وسط البلد/ فندق ...	**hæ**zæl '**inwæ**n/**wa**sat il bælæd/**fon**dok
Turn left/right at the next corner.	الى الشمال / اليمين فى الشارع القادم .	ilæ æsh**shi**mæl/æl yæmin fil **shæ**ri' æl **kā**dim
Go straight ahead.	استمر الى الامام .	istæ**mirr** ilæl æ**mæ**m
Stop here, please.	قف هنا من فضلك .	kiff **ho**næ min **fad**lak
I'm in a hurry.	أنا مستعجل .	ænæ mis**ta'**gil
Could you drive more slowly?	من فضلك سق على مهلك .	min **fad**lak sūk ælæ **mæh**læk
Could you help to carry my bags?	من فضلك ساعدنى فى حمل شنطى .	min **fad**lak sæ'**id**ni fi ḥæml **sho**nati

FOR TIPPING, see inside back-cover

Hotel—Other accommodation

Early reservation (and confirmation) is essential in most major tourist centres during the high season. You may have to pay a supplementary charge on Islamic high holidays.

فندق (**fondok**) Hotel. There's no official classification of hotels in the Middle East, but you'll find those of the highest international standards as well as others which seem to have no standards at all! You'd be well advised to choose a hotel with care, thus avoiding any unpleasant surprise. Your travel agent or the local tourist office usually has a list of hotels in three or more price categories.

بنسيون (**pænsyōn**) Boarding house. Generally occupying a floor of an apartment block, boarding houses are found in most towns. Prices are reasonable, and service is good. If you plan to stay a week or so, ask the manager for a reduction.

شقق مفروشة (**shokæk mæfrūshæ**) Furnished flats (apartments). Found particularly in Cairo and Beirut, such accommodation is cheap and practical for longer stays (several weeks).

بيت شباب (**bēt shæbæb**) Youth hostel. These are found in most Middle Eastern countries. Inquire at the local tourist office or at the Youth Hostels Association in your own country before leaving home.

In this section, we're mainly concerned with the smaller and medium-class hotels. You'll have no language difficulties in the luxury and first-class hotels where most of the staff can speak English.

In the next few pages we consider your basic requirements, step by step, from arrival to departure. You need not read all of it, just turn to the situation that applies.

Checking in—Reception

My name is…	اسمى ...	ismi
I have a reservation.	عندى حجز .	indi ḥægz
We've reserved 2 rooms, a single and a double.*	حجزنا غرفتين . غرفة لشخص وغرفة لشخصين .	**ḥægæ**znæ gorfa**tēn**. **gor**fa **lishakhs** wæ **gor**fa **lishakh**sēn
Here's the confirmation.	هذا تأكيد الحجز .	**hǣ**zæ **tæ**'kid æl ḥægz
I'd like a…	أريد ...	o**rid**
single room	غرفة لشخص	**gor**fa li**shakhs**
double room	غرفة لشخصين	**gor**fa li**shakh**sēn
suite	جناح	gæ**nǣh**
room with twin beds	غرفة بسريرين	**gor**fa bisi**rīrēn**
room with a bath	غرفة لها حمام	**gor**fa **læ**hǣ **ḥæm**mǣm
room with a shower	غرفة لها دوش	**gor**fa **læ**hǣ dosh
room with a balcony	غرفة لها بلكونة	**gor**fa **læ**hǣ bæl**kō**næ
room with a view	غرفة بها منظر جميل	**gor**fa **bi**hǣ **man**zar **gæ**mil
We'd like a room…	نريد غرفة ...	no**rid gor**fa
in the front	فى الأمام	fil æ**mǣm**
at the back	فى الخلف	fil **khælf**
facing the sea	تطل على البحر	to**till** 'ælæl **baḥr**
facing the gardens	تطل على الحديقة	to**till** 'ælæl ḥæ**di**ka

* see grammar

FOR NUMBERS, see page 175

It must be quiet.	لا بد أن تكون هادئة .	**læ**bodd æn tæ**kūn hæ**di'æ
Is there…?	هل يوجد ... ؟	hæll **yū**gæd
air conditioning	تكييف هواء	tækyif **hæ**wæ
heating	تدفئة	tæd**fi**'æ
a radio/television in the room	راديو / تليفزيون فى الغرفة	**rad**yo/tili**visy**ōn fil **gor**fa
a laundry	غسيل ومكوة	gæ**sīl** wæ **mæk**wæ
room service	خدمة فى الغرفة	**khid**mæ fil **gor**fa
hot water	ماء ساخن	mæ' **sæ**khin
running water	ماء جارى	mæ' **gæ**ri
a private toilet	تواليت خاص	twæ**litt** khās

How much?

What's the price…?	كم الثمن ... ؟	kæm æl **tæ**mæn
per night	لمدة يوم	li**mod**dit yōm
per week	لمدة أسبوع	li**mod**dit os**bū**
for bed and breakfast	للنوم والفطار	lil**nōm** wæl fi**tār**
excluding meals	بدون وجبات	bi**dūn** wæg**bæt**
for full board	للاقامة الكاملة	lil i**kā**mæ æl **kæ**milæ
for half board	لنصف الاقامة	li**nisf** æl 'i**kā**mæ
Does that include meals/service?	هل هذا يشمل الوجبات / الخدمة ؟	hæl **hæ**zæ **yæsh**mæl æl wæg**bæt**/æl **khid**mæ
Is there any reduction for children?	هل يوجد تخفيض للاطفال ؟	hæl **yū**gæd **takh**fid lil **at**fāl
Do you charge for the baby?	هل تحاسب على الطفل ؟	hæl to**ḥæ**sib 'ælæl tifl
That's too expensive.	هذا غالى جداً .	**hæ**zæ **gæ**li **gid**dæn
Haven't you anything cheaper?	هل عندك شيء أرخص ؟	hæl **in**dæk shē' **ar**khass

FOR NUMBERS, see page 175

How long?

We'll be staying…	... سنبقى	sænæbkā
overnight only	الليلة فقط	æl lēlæ fakatt
a few days	بضعة أيام	bid'at ǣyyæm
a week (at least)	أسبوع (على الأقل)	osbū (ælæl akall)
I don't know yet.	لا أعرف بعد .	læ āraf bæ'd

Decision

May I see the room?	أريد أن أرى الغرفة من فضلك	orīd æn aral gorfa min fadlak
No, I don't like it.	لا . انها لا تعجبني	læ. innæhæ læ to'gibni
It's too…	انها ... جداً .	innæhæ …giddæn
cold/hot	باردة / ساخنة	bǣridæ/sǣkhinæ
dark/small	ضلمة / صغيرة	dalma/sagīræ
noisy	دوشه	dæwshæ
I asked for a room with a bath.	طلبت غرفة بحمام .	talabt gorfa biḥæmmǣm
Have you anything…?	هل عندك شيء ... ؟	hæl indæk shē'
better/bigger	أحسن / أكبر	æḥsæn/akbar
cheaper/quieter	أرخص / أهدأ	arkhass/æhdæ'
That's fine. I'll take it.	كويس . سآخذها .	kwæyyis. sæ'ækhozhæ

Bills

Provided an extra room isn't required, there's often a reduction of 50 per cent in luxury and first-class hotels for children up to the age of six, and 30 per cent for 6–12 year-olds. Enquire about a similar arrangement at smaller hotels.

A service charge is normally included in the bill, but you can ask:

Is service included?	هل الخدمة محسوبة ؟	hæl æl khidmæ mæḥsūbæ

FOR TIPPING, see back-cover

Registration

On arrival at a hotel or boarding house you'll be asked to fill in a registration form. It asks your name, home address, passport number and further destination. It's almost certain to carry an English translation. If it doesn't, ask the desk clerk:

What does this mean?	ما معنى هذا ؟	mǣ **mæ**ænæ **hǣ**zæ

The desk clerk will probably ask you for your passport. He may want to keep it for a while, even overnight. Don't worry—you'll get it back. The desk clerk may want to ask you the following questions:

أريد أن أرى الباسبور من فضلك .	May I see your passport?
من فضلك املأ هذه الاستمارة .	Would you mind filling in this registration form?
من فضلك وقّـع هنا .	Sign here, please.
ما طول مدة اقامتك ؟	How long will you be staying?

What's my room number?	ما نمرة غرفتى ؟	mǣ **nim**rit gor**fa**ti
Will you have our bags sent up?	من فضلك ارسل الحقائب فوق .	min **fad**lak **ir**sil il ḥa**kā**'ib fōk
I'd like to leave this in your safe.	أريد أن أترك هذا فى الخزنة .	o**rīd** æn **æ**trok **hǣ**zæ fil **khæz**næ

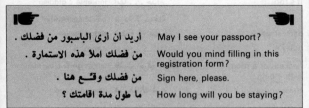

Service, please

Apart from maids, hotel staff in the Middle East is generally only composed of men.

maid	خادمة الغرفة	khæ**di**mæt æl **gor**fæ
manager	المدير	æl mo**dir**
room service	الخدمة فى الغرفة	æl **khid**mæ fil **gor**fæ
switchboard operator	عامل التليفون	**ǣ**mil il **tilifōn**

If you want to call the members of the staff, say: Please (min **fad**lak)!

General requirements

Please ask the maid to come up.	من فضلك اطلب من خادمة الغرفة أن تصعد .	min **fad**lak **ot**lob min khæ**di**mæt æl **gor**fæ æn **tas**'ad
Who is it?	مين ؟	min
Just a minute.	لحظة واحدة !	**la**ḥza **wæḥ**dæ
Come in!	أدخل !	**od**kholl
Is there a bath on this floor?	هل يوجد حمام فى هذا الطابق ؟	hæl **yū**gæd ḥæm**mǣm** fi **hǣ**zæl **tā**bik
Please send up…	من فضلك ارسل لنا ...	min **fad**lak **ir**sil **læ**nǣ
two coffees/a sandwich	فنجالين قهوة / سسندوتش	fingæ**lēn** æh**wæ**/ sændæ**witsh**
a bottle of mineral water	زجاجة مياه معدنية	zo**gǣ**git mi**yǣh** mæ'dæ**niy**yæ
Can we have breakfast in our room?	هل يمكن الافطار ق غرفتنا؟	hæl **yom**kin æl **'iftār** fi gor**fa**tinǣ
May I have a/an/some…?	من فضلك أريد ...	min **fad**lak o**rīd**
ashtray	طفاية سجاير	taf**fā**yit sæ**gǣ**yir
bath towel	فوطة حمام	**fū**tit hæm**mǣm**

extra blanket	بطانية زيادة	battaniyya ziy**ǣ**dæ
envelopes	ظروف	zorūf
(more) hangers	علاقات (زيادة)	æll**ǣ**kāt (ziy**ǣ**dæ)
hot-water bottle	قربة ماء ساخن	irbit mǣ' s**ǣ**khin
ice cubes	قطع ثلج	kita' tælg
needle and thread	ابرة وخيط	ibræ wæ khēt
extra pillow	مخدة زيادة	mæ**kh**æddæ ziy**ǣ**dæ
reading-lamp	لمبة للقراءة	lamba lil kirā'a
soap	صابون	sabūn
writing-paper	ورق للكتابة	wæræ' lil kit**ǣ**bæ
Where's the...?	أين يوجد ... ؟	æynæ yūgæd
bar	البار	æl bār
barber's	حلاق	ḥællāk
bathroom	الحمام	æl ḥæmm**ǣ**m
beauty salon	صالون التجميل	salōn æl tægmil
dining room	صالة الطعام	sālit æl ta'ām
restaurant	المطعم	æl mat'am
television room	صالة التليفزيون	sālit æl tilivisyōn
toilet	التواليت	æl twælitt

Breakfast

In the Middle East, breakfast consists of *fool* (black beans), white cheese, *halava* (a sugary confection) and *falafel* (fried balls of ground *fool*). If this doesn't suit your palate, most top-class hotels serve continental or American breakfasts.

I'll have a/an/some...	أريد. . . .	orīd
eggs	بيض	bēd
boiled egg	بيضة مسلوقة	bēda mæslu'æ
soft/medium/hard	نصف سواء/متوسط/ جـامد	nisf siwæ/motæ**wassit**/ g**ǣ**mid
fried egg	بيضة مقلية	bēda makliyya

fruit juice	عصير فاكهة	assīr fækihæ
grapefruit/orange	جريب فروت / برتقال	grēp frūt/bortokāl
pineapple/tomato	أنناس / طماطم	ænænǣs/tamātim
omelet	عجة	'igga
May I have some...?	أريد ... من فضلك	orīd...min fadlak
bread/toast	خبز / توست	khobz/tost
hot/cold milk	لبن ساخن / لبن بارد	læbæn sǣkhin/ læbæn bǣrid
cream/sugar	كريم / سكر	krēm/sokkar
more butter	زبد زيادة	zibdæ ziyǣdæ
salt/pepper	ملح / فلفل	mælḥ/filfil
coffee/tea	قهوة / شاى	æhwæ/shǣy
hot chocolate	شكولاتة ساخنة	shokolāta sokhnæ
lemon/honey	ليمون / عسل	læmūn/æsæl
jam/marmalade	مربى / مربى برتقال	marabba/marabbit bortokāl
Could you bring me a...	من فضلك احضرلى ...	min fadlak iḥdir li
plate	صحن	sahn
glass	كباية	kobbǣyæ
cup	فنجان	fingǣn
knife	سكينة	sikkīnæ
fork	شوكة	shōkæ
spoon	ملعقة	mil'aka

Difficulties

The ... doesn't work.	ال ... لا يعمل .	il...lǣ yæ'mæl
air conditioner	تكييف الهواء	tækyīf hæwǣ
fan	مروحة	marwaḥa
light	نور	nūr
tap	صنبور [حنفية]	sonbūr [ḥænæfiyyæ]
toilet	تواليت	twælitt

FOR EATING OUT, see pages 38–64

The wash basin is blocked.	الحوض مسدود .	æl ḥōd mæsdūd
The window is jammed.	الشباك من الصعب فتحه.	æl shibbǣk min æl saab fæthọ
The blind is stuck.	الغمامات لا تعمل .	æl gæmæmǣt læ tææmæl
These aren't my shoes.	هذا ليس حذائى .	hǣzæ læysæ ḥizǣ'i
This isn't my laundry.	هذا ليس غسيلى .	hǣzæ læysæ gæsīli
There's no hot water.	لا يوجد ماء ساخن .	lǣ yūgæd mǣ' sǣkhin
I've lost my watch.	ساعتى ضاعت .	sǣ'æti dā'it
I've left my key in my room.	لقد تركت المفتاح فى غرفتى .	tarakt æl moftǣḥ fi gorfati
The bulb is burnt out.	لمبة النور محروقة .	lambit æl nūr mæḥrūka
The ... is broken.	الـ ... مكسور .	æl...maksūr
lamp	مصباح	misbāḥ
plug	كبس	kobs
shutter/window shade	شيش / غمامات	shīsh/gæmmæmǣt
switch	مفتاح النور	moftǣḥ æl nūr
Can you get it fixed?	هل يمكن اصلاحها ؟	hæl yomkin islāḥihǣ

Telephone—Mail—Callers

Can you get me Cairo 123456?	أريد الاتصال بالقاهرة رقم ١٢٣٤٥٦ .	orīd æl 'ittisāl bil kāhira rakam 12 34 56
Did anyone telephone me?	هل اتصل بى أحد تليفونيا؟	hæl ittasala bi 'æḥæd tilifōniyyæn
Is there any mail for me?	هل توجد خطابات لى؟	hæl tūgæd khitabǣt li
Have you any stamps?	هل عندك طوابع بريد ؟	hæl ændæk tawābi' bærīd
Would you please mail this for me?	هل يمكنك ارسال هذا بالبريد ؟	hæl yomkinæk irsǣl hǣza bil bærīd
Are there any messages for me?	هل توجد رسالة لى؟	hæl tūgæd risǣlæ li

FOR POST OFFICE AND TELEPHONE, see page 137

Checking out

May I have my bill, please? Room 398.	أريد فاتورة حسابى من فضلك غرفة رقم ٣٩٨.	orīd fatūrit ḥisæbi min **fad**lak. **gor**fæ **ra**kam 398
I'm leaving early tomorrow.	سأرحل مبكراً صباح الغد .	sæ'**ar**ḥal mobæk**kiran** sa**bāḥ** æl gædd
Please have my bill ready.	من فضلك جهز لى الفاتورة.	min **fad**lak gæh**hiz**lī æl fa**tū**ra
We'll be checking out around noon.	سنرحل حوالى الظهر .	sæ**nar**ḥal ḥa**wæ**lī æl zohr
I must leave at once.	لا بد أن أرحل فوراً .	**læbodd** æn **ar**ḥal **faw**ran
Does this include service?	هل هذا يشمل الخدمة ؟	hæl **hæ**zæ **yæsh**mæl æl **khid**mæ
Is everything included?	هل كل شيء محسوب ؟	hæl koll shē' mæḥ**sūb**
You've made a mistake in this bill, I think.	أظن أنك أخطات فى حساب هذه الفاتورة .	a**zonn** 'ænnækæ akh**ta't** fi ḥi**sæb** hæzihi æl fatūra
Can you get us a taxi?	من فضلك اطلب لنا تاكسى .	min **fad**lak **ot**lob **læ**næ **tæk**si
When's the next... to Cairo?	متى موعد ... القادم الى القاهرة ؟	mæ**tæ maw'**id æl..æl **kā**dim ilæ ælkā**hi**ra
bus/train/plane	الأوتوبيس / القطار / الطائرة	æl 'oto**bīs**/æl ki**tār**/ æl **tā'**ira
Would you send someone to bring down our baggage?	من فضلك ارسل أحداً لانزال الحقائب .	min **fad**lak **ir**sil 'æḥædæn li'in**zæl** æl ḥa**kā'**ib
We're in a great hurry.	اننا فى غاية الاستعجال .	in**næ**næ fi **gā**yæt æl '**isti'**gæl
Here's the forwarding address. You have my home address.	هذا هو عنواننا القادم . عندك عنوان منزلى .	**hæ**zæ **ho**wæ inwæ**no**næ æl **kā**dim. **in**dæk inn**wæn** mæ**n**zili
It's been a very enjoyable stay.	كانت الاقامة ممتعة جداً .	**kæ**næt æl '**ikā**ma momti'æ **gid**dæn

FOR TAXI, see page 27

HOTEL SERVICE

Eating out

There are many types of places where you can eat and drink in the Arab countries.

مطعم (mat'am)	A restaurant; there's often a set menu, especially in European ones.
حـاتي (ḥāāti)	A restaurant specializing in charcoal-grilled lamb.
مطعم لحم مشوى (mat'am laḥm mæshwi)	Same as the above, only the name is different in Lebanon.
مطعم حمام (mat'am ḥæmāām)	A restaurant specializing in pigeon or squab
مطعم سمك (mat'am sæmæk)	Fish and seafood restaurant.
فول وفلافل (fūl wæ fælāāfil)	A snack-bar; this is a popular type of eating place serving *fool* (black-bean dish) and *falafel* (small balls of ground black beans, fried and served with a choice of spices). *Fool* and *falafel* may also be a filling for sandwiches.
كافيتريا (kæfitiryæ)	A snack-bar; you may have to eat standing up.
محـل عصير (mæḥæl 'asīr)	Fruit-juice bar (sometimes it's a drive-in); features fresh fruit juice. Often you can get *shawerma*—thin slices of spitroasted lamb—and sandwiches.
صالون شاى (salōn shǣy)	A coffee shop; it's often a part of a pastry shop.
حلويـات شامى (ḥælæwiyyǣt shǣmi)	A Lebanese or Syrian pastry shop.
ملهى ليـلى (mælhǣ læyli)	Night-club (cabaret); dinner and a show; in Egypt all the shows feature the famed belly dancers whom you won't want to miss.

كاس عرق ومـازة (kǣs 'arak wæ mǣzæ) A restaurant in Lebanon which serves salads and appetizers among other local dishes. This type of restaurant traditionally serves *arak*, an aniseed liqueur and the national drink, as beverage.

There are also neighbourhood restaurants, many of which specialize in a particular dish such as *kosharee* (rice, lentils and hot sauce), *kebda wa mokh* (liver and brains) or *fiseekh* (dried fish).

Eating habits

In this section we're primarily concerned with restaurants—and with lunch and dinner. We assume that you've already had breakfast at your hotel.

In the Arab countries, meals are generally eaten later than at home—both privately and in restaurants.

غـذاء (gædæ) Lunch is generally served from 1 to 3 p.m.

عشـاء ('æshæ) Dinner is served from 8 to 11 p.m. In night-clubs you'll be able to dine even after midnight.

If you feel hungry at an unusual hour, you'll always be able to find a restaurant or a snack-bar serving warm dishes or snacks at any time of the day or night.

Most large restaurants in major cities specialize in European dishes, especially French and Italian, rather than Middle Eastern cuisine. But you'll usually find some Middle Eastern dishes on the menu. Unless you're specifically looking for European food, avoid the big restaurants and go to local eating places.

In summer many restaurants as well as night-clubs move outdoors to take advantage of the fine weather.

FOR BREAKFAST, see page 34

What is Ramadan?

The month of Ramadan is one of Islam's holy periods. As it's a lunar month, it has no regular corresponding date in the calendar year. It's observed by Moslems in all Arab countries by fasting and by refraining from drinking and smoking from sunrise to sunset. This religious rite is a way of showing one's obedience to God and of strengthening social relations.

The main meal of the day which is taken at sunset is called *iftar*. It usually starts with a hot soup, then goes on with *fool* and eggs, generally mixed together, and the rest of the meal is a normal one, followed by oriental sweets. The characteristic drink of this month (non-alcoholic, of course) is *kamar-eldin*. It's made of a stewed apricot purée which is served fresh. Just try it and you'll surely ask for more.

Iftar provides the opportunity to meet friends and relatives; it's also a time of charity when beggars, who knock at the door at this special period of the year, will be given food. After *iftar,* people usually listen to music and to readings from the Koran on the radio and go to the mosque. Restaurants and cafés stay open all night and are well patronized.

Later on, at about 1 or 2 a.m., you take your second meal of the "day", called *sohur,* which helps the Moslem to endure the long hours of fasting to come.

During Ramadan, public places are open all night and the streets are brightly illuminated. Nevertheless, one shouldn't forget that the month of Ramadan is first and foremost a religious month.

But don't worry: non-Moslem visitors aren't expected to fast. You'll find eating places open specially for you.

Hungry

I'm hungry/I'm thirsty.	أنا جوعان / أنا عطشان .	'ænæ gæ'ǣn/'ænæ 'atshān
Can you recommend a good (and inexpensive) restaurant?	من فضلك انصحني بمطعم جيد (ورخيص) .	min fadlak 'insaḥni bimat'am gæyyid (wæ rakhīs)
I'd like to reserve a table for 4.	أريد أن أحجز ترابيزة [طاولة] لـ ٤ .	orīd æn 'æḥgiz tarabēza [tawla] li 4
We'll come at 8.	سنأتى الساعة ٨ .	sænæ'ti æl sǣæ 8

Asking and ordering

Could we have a...?	من فضلك نريد ...	min fadlak norīd
table in the corner	ترابيزة [طاولة] منعزلة	tarabēza [tawla] mon'æzilæ
table by the window	ترابيزة [طاولة] بجانب الشباك	tarabēza [tawla] bigǣnib æl shibbǣk
table outside	ترابيزة [طاولة] فى الخارج	tarabēza [tawla] fil khǣrig
What's the price of the set menu?	ما هو ثمن الوجبة ؟	mǣ howæ tæmæn æl wægbæ
Is service included?	هل الخدمة محسوبة ؟	hæl æl khidmæ mæḥsūbæ
Could we have a(n) ... please?	من فضلك نريد ...	min fadlak norīd
ashtray	طفاية سجاير [منفضة]	taffāyit sægǣyir [manfada]
finger bowl	كأس ماء لغسل الأصابع	kǣs mayya ligæsl æl'asābi'
fork	شوكة	shōkæ
glass	كباية	kobbǣyæ
knife	سكينة	sikkīnæ
plate	صحن	saḥn
serviette (napkin)	فوطة	fūta
spoon	ملعقة	mal'aka
tablecloth	مغرش سفرة	mafrash sofra
toothpick	مسلكة أسنان	mæslækit 'æsnǣn

FOR COMPLAINTS, see page 59

I'd like a/an/some…	أريد …	orīd
beer	بيرة	bīræ
bread	عيش [خبز]	'ēsh [khobz]
butter	زبدة	zibdæ
cheese	جبنة	gibnæ
chips (french fries)	شيبس	ships
coffee	قهوة	'æhwæ
fish	سمك	sæmæk
fowl	دجاج	dægæ̈g
fruit	فاكهة	fækhæ
ice-cream	جلاس [بوظة]	glæs [būza]
lemon	ليمون [حامض]	læymūn [ḥāmid]
lettuce	خس	khass
meat	لحم	læḥm
milk	لبن حليب	læbæn ḥælīb
mineral water	مياه معدنية	mayya mæ'dæniyyæ
mustard	مستردة [خردل]	mostarda [khærdæl]
noodles	مكرونة شريط	makarōna shirīt
olive oil	زيت زيتون	zēt zætūn
pepper	فلفل [بهار]	filfil [bohār]
potatoes	بطاطس	batātis
rice	رز	roz
rolls	خبز سندوتش	khobz sændæwitsh
salad	صلطة	salata
salt	ملح	mælḥ
sandwich	سندوتش	sændæwitsh
soup	شوربة	shorba
sugar	سكر	sokkar
tea	شاى	shæ̈y
vegetables	خضار	khodār
vinegar	خل	khæl
(iced) water	مياه (مثلجة)	mayya (mitælligæ)
wine	نبيذ	nibīt

What's on the menu

Our menu is presented according to courses. Under each heading you'll find an alphabetical list of dishes in Arabic with their English equivalents. This list—which includes everyday and special dishes—will enable you to make the most of an Arabic menu.

Here's our guide to good eating and drinking. Turn to the course you want to start with.

Arab cooking is in many ways typical of what you'll find throughout the Mediterranean. Many popular dishes of Egypt, for example, have been inherited from the Turks or the Circassians, a Moslem people who emigrated from Russia in the last century. Much emphasis is placed on grilling or slowly braising vegetable or meat stews.

Appetizers—Starters

It's customary in Arab countries to serve a variety of appetizers and salads with the aperitif. These are called the *mezza*. This consists of numerous small plates of hors d'œuvre. Lebanon is especially noted for the diversity and tastiness of its *mezza*. A complete one consists of about 40 different appetizers. We don't have room to name them all, but here's a sampling of some popular ones.

I'd like an appetizer.	أريد فاتح شهية من فضلك .	orīd **fǣ**tiḥ shæ**hiy**yæ min **fad**lak

أنشوجـة	'æn**shū**gæ	anchovies
اسبرجس	'asparagas	asparagus tips
خرشوف [أرضى شوكى]	khar**shūf** ['**ar**dī **shō**kī]	artichokes
بيـض	bēd	eggs
بيض بالمايونيز	bēd bil mæyo**nēz**	egg salad
رنجـة	ringæ	herring
رنجـة مملحة	ringæ momæl**læ**ḥæ	salted-herring fillets
زيتــون	zæ**tūn**	olives
مخللات [كبيس]	mikhælli**lǣt** [kæ**bīs**]	pickles (pickled vegetables)
كبـد الوز	kæbid æl**wiz**	goose-liver pâté
كبـد دجاج	kæbid dæ**gǣg**	chopped chicken liver
عصير فاكهـة	'asīr fækhæ	fruit juice
شمــام	shæm**mǣm**	melon
ســلامى	sæ**lǣ**mi	salami
سجق [مقــانق]	**sogo'** [mæ'**ǣ**nik]	sausages
سردين	sær**dīn**	sardines
كركنـد	kara**kænd**	lobster
باتيـه [فواجرا]	**pǣ**t**ēh** [fwa**grā**]	pâté
جندفلى [محــار]	**gæn**do**flī** [ma**ḥḥār**]	oysters
كافيــار	kav**yār**	caviar

Arabic specialities

باذنجان مخلـل (bitin**gæn** mikh**æ**llil)	aubergine (eggplant) stuffed with herbs, garlic and spices.
ورق عنب محشي (wæræ' 'inæb **mæ**ḥshi)	grape leaves stuffed with rice and minced meat; may be served cold or hot.
طحينـة (ti**ḥī**na)	a paste made with ground sesame seeds and spices; particularly good with fish.
بابـا غنوج (babagæn**nūg**)	*tehina* to which mashed aubergine (eggplant) is added.
حمص بطحينـة (**ḥo**mmos bit**ḥī**na)	a spicy paste made with ground chick-peas, *tehina* and spices.
جبنة بيضاء بالطماطم (**gib**næ **bē**da bil tam**ā**tim)	white cheese served with tomatoes, onion, parsley, oil and lemon; sometimes a hot sauce is added.
بطـارخ (bat**ā**rikh)	"Egyptian caviar", red fish roe
عجـة ('**ig**gæ)	omelet, made of onions, parsley and green pepper; baked.

Salads

What salads do you have?	ما أصناف الصلاطة عندكم ؟	mæ 'as**nāf** ælsa**la**ta æn**do**kom
صلاطة خيـار وطماطم [بندورة]	sa**la**tit khi**yār** wæ ta**mā**tim [bana**dū**ra]	cucumber and tomato salad
صلاطة بطاطس	sa**la**tit ba**tā**tis	potato salad
صلاطـة كرفس	sa**la**tit ka**rafs**	celery salad
صلاطـة خس	sa**la**tit khass	lettuce salad
صلاطة باذنجـان	sa**la**tit bitin**gæn**	aubergine (eggplant) salad
صلاطة بنجر [شمندر]	sa**la**tit **ban**gar	beetroot salad
صلاطـة جرجير	sa**la**tit gær**gīr**	watercress salad

EATING OUT

Salad specialities

Can you recommend a local speciality?	من فضلك انصحنى بأكلة محلية .	min **fad**lak 'insaḥnī bi 'æklæ mæḥælliyyæ

لبن زبادى وخيار (læbæn zæ**bæ**dī wæ khi**yār**)	diced cucumbers with a dressing of yogurt, olive oil, garlic and mint leaves
صلاطة بلدى (salata bælædi)	salad of cucumbers, tomatoes, onions, watercress, parsley, green peppers, mint leaves (Egypt)
تبولة (tæbb**ū**læ)	Lebanese salad, similar to the Egyptian one, but with cracked wheat and bread crumbs

Cheese

In Arab countries a lot of cheese is eaten, and it's eaten with the meal, not after the main course. Moreover, it's served most frequently with breakfast and supper. You'll also find it served under various guises as a part of the *mezza*, or appetizers.

جبنة بيضاء من لبن معيز (**gib**næ **bē**da min læbæn mi'īz)	white goat's milk cheese
جبنة مالحة (**gib**næ **mæl**ḥæ)	salted fresh-curd cheese
جبنة أريش (gibnæ 'ærīsh)	full, rich cheese, slightly salty
جبنة ريكوتا (gibnæ rikotta)	a type of cottage cheese
مش (mesh)	well aged, very salty and sharp
لبنة (læbnæ)	a fresh-curd cheese sprinkled with olive oil

Soup

You'll find many different kinds of soup in the Middle East, among them many European and American favourites as well as regional specialities. Lentil soup is the most popular of the local soups.

I'd like some soup.	أريد شوربة من فضلك .	orīd **shor**ba min **fad**lak
What do you recommend?	بم تنصح ؟	**bi**mæ **tan**saḥ

شوربة عدس	**shor**bit 'æds	lentil soup
شوربة فراخ [دجاج]	**shor**bit fi**rǣkh**	chicken soup
شوربة لحم	**shor**bit læḥm	meat soup
شوربة باذلاء	**shor**bit bisillæ	pea soup
شوربة خضار	**shor**bit khodār	vegetable soup
شوربة سمك	**shor**bit sæmæk	fish soup
شوربة بصل	**shor**bit basal	onion soup
شوربة طماطم [بندورة]	**shor**bit tamātim [banadūra]	tomato soup
شوربة شعرية	**shor**bit shi'riyyæ	noodle soup
شوربة عدس بحامض	**shor**bit 'æds biḥāmid	lentil and lemon soup (Lebanon)

Fish and seafood

Alexandria and Beirut are especially good places to sample fish and seafood, and you'll want to try the grilled shrimps. Aboukir is a fishing village near Alexandria where you can taste the catch fresh from the Mediterranean. If you're lucky, a fisherman may suggest grilling a fish for you right at the seaside. In Cairo, you're likely to eat fish from the Nile. Very often you'll find there is a fishmonger's attached to the restaurant. Consequently you can be sure of having fresh fish and can even pick the one you want for dinner.

I'd like some fish.	أريد سمكاً من فضلك .	orīd sæmæk min fadlak
What kinds of seafood do you have?	أى أصناف السمك عندكم ؟	'æyy 'asnāf æl sæmæk 'ændokom

In addition to a lot of exotic local fish, here are the names of a few more common varieties:

أنشوجة	ænshūgæ	anchovies
استاكوزا [كركند]	istækōzæ [kæræ kænd]	lobster
جمبرى [قرادس]	gæmbæri ['æræ̃dis]	shrimp
جندفلى [محار]	gændofli [maḥḥār]	oysters
كابوريا	kæboryæ	crab
سردين	særdīn	sardines
تونة	tūnæ	tunny (tuna)
سمك موسى	sæmæk mūsæ	sole

Some of the ways you may want your fish served:

baked	فى الفرن	fil forn
cured	مملح	momællæḥ
fried	مقلى	mæ'lī
grilled	مشوى	mæshwi
marinated	متبَّل	motæbbæl
poached	مسلوق	mæslū'
smoked	مدخن	modækhkhæn
steamed	بالبخار	bil bokhār

كباب سمك (kæbæ̃b sæmæk)	chunks of fish, stewed and charcoal grilled with pieces of tomatoes and green pepper
سمك صيادية (sæmæk sayyadiyyæ)	chunks of fish cooked in oil and served with rice flavoured with the fish cooking oil

EATING OUT

Meat

Eating pork is forbidden according to Moslem dietary laws, therefore it's rarely found on a menu.

What kinds of meat do you have?	أى أصناف اللحم عندكم ؟	'ævy 'asn**ā**f ællæḥm 'ændokom
I'd like some...	أريد لحم ...	or**ī**d læḥm
beef/veal/lamb	بقرى/بتلو/ضانى	bæ'æri/bitillo/d**ā**ni

أوزى	'**ū**zi	baby lamb
ريش [كستليتة] ضانى	riyæsh [kostæl**ē**tæ] d**ā**ni	lamb chops
لسان	lis**æ**n	tongue
اسكالوب	'iskælop	scallop
جامبون – خنزير	zhæmb**ō**n-khænz**ī**r	ham
كوارع بتلو	kæwæri' bitillo	calf's trotters (feet)
لحم مفروم	læḥm mafr**ū**m	minced meat
كستليتة	kostæl**ē**tæ	cutlets
موزة	m**ō**zæ	shank, knuckle
سجق [مقانق]	sogo' [mæ'**ǣ**nik]	sausages
كستليتة بتلو [عجل]	kostæl**ē**tæ bitillo ['igl]	veal chops
بفتيك	boft**ē**k	beef steak
فخذ (ضانى)	fækhdæ (d**ā**ni)	leg (of lamb)
مخ	mokh	brains
كلاوى	kæl**ǣ**wi	kidneys
كتف	kitf	shoulder
روسبيف	rozb**ī**f	roast beef
رأس [نيفة]	r**ā**s [n**ī**fæ]	head
رقبة	ræ'æbæ	neck
فيلتو	filitto	fillet
صدر	sidr	breast
كبدة	kibdæ	liver
كفتة	koftæ	meatballs
كرشة	kirshæ	tripe

Arabic meat dishes

كباب (kæbææb)	spicy chunks of charcoal-grilled lamb
ريش (riyæsh)	spicy charcoal-grilled lamb chops
كفتة (koftæ)	charcoal-grilled minced meatballs
شاورمة (shawirmæ)	chunks of lamb roasted on a vertical spit from which thin slices are cut and served either in a bun or on a plate, usually with rice; a popular snack served from roadside stands
كبيبة [كبة] (kobēbæ [kibbæ])	minced meat, cracked wheat, onion, baked in butter; it can be served raw *(kobeiba naya)*, baked *(kobeiba besseniyah)* or rolled into dumplings and served in goat's milk soup *(kobeiba labniyeh)* (Lebanon)
مقلوبة (mæ'lūbæ)	meat and aubergine (eggplant) served with rice
فتة (fættæ)	boiled mutton and rice mixed with bread crumbs and broth, served with vinegar and garlic
صفيحة (sfiḥæ)	a pastry crust like pizza garnished with seasoned minced mutton (Lebanon)

barbecued	مشوى على الفحم	mæshwi 'ælæl fæḥm
fried	مقلى	mæ'li
grilled	مشوى	mæshwi
roasted	رستو	rosto
stewed	مسلوق	mæslū'
stuffed	محشى	mæḥshi
underdone (rare)	قليل السواء	kalīl ælsiwæ
medium	نصف سواء	nisf siwæ
well-done	مستوى	mistiwi

Game and fowl

I'd like some game. أريد طيور . orīd toyūr

أرنب	'ærnæb	rabbit
بط	batt	duck
بط برّي	batt **bærri**	wild duck
حمام	hæmǣm	pigeon
ديك رومي [حبشي]	dīk rūmi [ḥæbæsh]	turkey
سمان [سمّن]	simmǣn [sommon]	quail
فراخ [فراريج]	firǣkh [frǣrīzh]	chicken
ورك/صدر/كبدة	wirk/sidr/**kibdæ**	leg/breast/liver
فراخ [فراريج] مشوية	firǣkh [frǣrizh] mæshwiyyæ	roast chicken
وز	wizz	goose

Game and poultry dishes

فراخ شركسية (**firǣkh** shærkæ**siyyæ**)	boiled chicken served with boiled rice and a sauce made of chopped walnuts, chili pepper and bread
فراخ بالخلطة (**firǣkh** bil **khalta**)	roast chicken served with rice mixed with nuts, chicken liver and giblets
كشك بالفراخ (kishk bil **firǣkh**)	pieces of boiled chicken braised in a gravy made of yogurt, chicken broth, onion and butter
حمام محشي أرز/فريك (hæ**mǣm mæḥ**shi roz/ **firik**)	pigeon stuffed with cracked wheat or seasoned rice
برام حمام (bi**rǣm** ḥæ**mǣm**)	pigeon baked in a casserole with rice and milk (Egypt)

Vegetables

What vegetables do you recommend? بای ّ الخضروات تنصح ؟ bi'æyy ælkhodrawāt tænsaḥ

أرز	roz	rice
باذنجان	bitingææn	aubergine (eggplant)
باميـة	bæmyæ	okra
باذلاء [بسلـة]	bisillæ	peas
بصـل	basal	onions
بطاطس	batātis	potatoes
ثـوم	tōm	garlic
جرجير	gærgīr	watercress
جزر	gazar	carrots
حمص	hommos	chick-peas
خرشوف [أرضى شوكى]	kharshūf [ardī shōkī]	artichoke
خس	khass	lettuce
خيـار	khiyār	cucumber
ذرة	dora	Indian corn
سبانخ	sæbææ̃nikh	spinach
طرشى [كبيس]	torshī [kæbīs]	gherkins
طماطم [بندورة]	tamātim [banadūra]	tomatoes
عـدس	'æds	lentils
فاصوليـا	fasolya	beans
لوبيا/خضراء/فول	lobyæ/khadra/fūl	string/green/black
فريـك	firīk [borgol]	cracked wheat
فجـل	figl	radishes
فلفـل أخضر	filfil akhdar	green peppers
قنبيط (أرنبيط)	arnabit	cauliflower
كرفس	karafs	celery
كرنب [ملفوف]	koromb [mælfūf]	cabbage
ورق عنب	wæræ' 'inæb	grape leaves

EATING OUT

Vegetables may be served:

baked	فى الفرن	fil forn
boiled	مسلوق	**mæslū'**
chopped	مخرط	mi**kh**arrat
creamed	بالصلصة البيضاء	bil **sal**sa ælb**ē**da
diced	مكعبات	mokæ'æ **bæ̈t**
fried	مقلى	**mæ**'li
grilled	مشوى	**mæsh**wi
roasted	رستو	**ros**to
stewed	مسلوق	mosæ**bb**æk
stuffed	محشى	**mæḥ**shi

Vegetable dishes

ملوخيـة (molo**khi**yyæ) A very popular Egyptian dish is a spicy soup of greens flavoured with garlic. It's usually made with rice and chicken or meat.

مسقعـة (mosæk**kæ**'æ) Fried aubergine (eggplant) cooked with meat and raisins

محشى (**mæḥ**shi) There's a variety of vegetables which fall into the category of *mahshees.* These are stuffed with a mixture of chopped meat (usually lamb or mutton), rice, onion and herbs. The most popular *mahshees* are the ones with grape leaves, green peppers, cabbage leaves, marrows (US zucchini), tomatoes and aubergine (eggplant). They can be eaten hot or cold and are usually served with yogurt.

لوبيـا بزيت (**lū**byæ bz**ē**t) Green beans fried in oil, then braised in tomato sauce and served chilled with lemon (Lebanon)

باميـة بالموزة (**bæm**yæ bil **mō**zæ) Okra braised in tomato sauce with beef knuckle

Fool

Fool is doubtless the favourite food preparation in the Middle East; its widespread popularity and its price put it on par with a hot-dog. *Fool* consists of black beans which have been cooked the previous night, seasoned with oil and lemon juice or served with butter. It may be served on a plate or in a bun. If you're in a hurry, stop at any *fool* restaurant and buy a *fool* or *falafel* sandwich.

فلافـل (fælæfil)	small balls of ground fool, mixed with greens and spices, fried in oil
بسارة (bisāra)	a purée made of ground fool, cooked with butter, and served with fried onions

Fool may also be eaten with Arab bread. Made of wheat- and Indian corn-flour, this tasty, flat, round bread replaces eating with utensils as it's used to scoop up food right from the bowl or plate.

Seeds, nuts, dried fruit

A major pastime in the Middle East seems to be cracking seeds. They're sold everywhere—near stadiums, at the cinema, on the streets and in the markets. The most common seed is from a variety of melon. Vendors of dried seeds also offer a choice of nuts and dried fruit.

dried seeds	محمصات	moḥammasāt
chestnuts	أبو فروة [كاستنة]	'æbū farwa [kæstænæ]
pecans	بكـان	pikkǣn
hazelnuts	بنـدق	bondo'
nuts	جـوز	gōz
walnuts	عين جمـل	'ēn gæmæl
pistachio	فستق	fosto'
peanuts	فول سودانى	fūl sūdǣni
almonds	لـوز	lōz

Fruit

The mild climate permits the cultivation of most of the fruit known in Europe as well as those from the tropics.

Do you have fresh fruit?	هل عندكم فواكه طازة؟	hæl ændokom fæwækih tāza

أنانـاس	'ænænæs	pineapple
برتقال [ليمون]	borto'æn [læymūn]	orange
برقوق [خوخ]	bær'ū' [khōkh]	plums
بطيخ	battikh	watermelon
بلح	bælæh	dates
تفـاح	tiffæh	apples
تين	tīn	figs
جريب فروت	grēb frūt	grapefruit
جوافـة	gæwæfæ	guava
جوز هندى	gōz hind	coconut
خوخ [دراء]	khōkh [darrā']	peach
رمـان	rommān	pomegranates
زبيب	zibīb	raisins
شمـام	shæmmæm	melon
عنب (بنـاتى)	'inæb (bænæti)	(seedless) grapes
فراولة	frawla	strawberries
قشطـة خضراء	'ishta khadra	custard apple, papaw
كـريز	krēz	cherries
كمثرى [نجاص]	kommitræ [nzhās]	pear
ليمون [حامض]	læmūn [ḥāmid]	lime
ليمون حلو	læmūn ḥilw	sweet lemon
مـانجة	mængæ	mangoes
مشمش	mishmish	apricots
مـوز	mōz	banana
يوسفندى [أفندى]	yosæfændi ['æfændī]	tangerines

Dessert

If you've survived all the courses on the menu, you may want to say:

I'd like a dessert, please.	أريد حلوا من فضلك .	orīd ḥilw min fadlak
Something light, please.	شيء خفيف من فضلك .	shē' khæfīf min fadlak
Just a small portion.	مقدار صغير .	mikdār sagīr
Nothing more, thanks.	لا شيء آخر ، شكراً .	læ shē' 'ākhar shokran

If you aren't sure what to order, ask the waiter:

What do you have for dessert?	أى حلويات عندكم ؟	'æyy hælæwiyyæt ændokom
What do you recommend?	بم تنصح ؟	bimæ tansaḥ
cake	كيك	kēk
caramel custard	كريم كراميل	krēm karamil
fruit salad	فروت سالاد	frūt salad
ice-cream	أيس كريم	'æys krim
rice pudding	أرز بلبن	roz bilæbæn
water-ice (sherbet)	جرانيطة [بوظة]	grānita [būza]

Arabs have a sweet tooth for gooey, syrupy desserts like the well-known *baklava*. Some desserts even bear such fascinating names as Lady's Navel and Ali's Mother. These desserts are usually served with cream. If not, you can ask for your dessert:

with cream	بقشطة	bi'ishta

Here are some favourite Arabic desserts:

بسيمة (bæsīmæ)	semolina pudding baked with coconut and sugar

بقلاوة (bæklǣwæ)	thin layers of pastry, filled with nuts, almonds and pistachios, steeped in syrup
بلح الشام (bælæḥ ishshǣm)	"Syria's dates": puff pastry, fried, steeped in syrup
خشاف (khoshǣf)	stewed fruit
صرة الست (sorrit issit)	"lady's navel": a ring-shaped sweet, steeped in syrup
عيش السراى ('ēsh æl sarāyæ)	"palace bread": deep-fried sweet roll, steeped in syrup
قرع عسلى (kar' 'æsæli)	pumpkin pudding with nuts, covered with a vanilla sauce; may be served hot or chilled
قطايف (katāyif)	a pastry filled with nuts, fried and then topped with syrup
كل واشكر (kol woshkor)	"eat it and thank God": smaller version of *baklava,* with less crust and more nuts, steeped in syrup
كنافة (konǣfæ)	pastry of thin fibres, baked with nuts or cream, steeped in syrup
أم على (om ali)	"Ali's mother", named after an Egyptian Mameluke queen; raisin cake, steeped in milk
بسبوسة (bæsbūsæ)	semolina tart, baked with butter, covered with syrup
مهلبية (mæhællæbiyyæ)	rice or Indian corn-flour pudding
ملبن [لكوم] (mælbæn [lokūm])	Turkish delight

After a dinner including dessert and fruit, Arabs like to drink a cup of Turkish coffee. You'll certainly want to sample this world-renowned brew which will probably be the only type of coffee you'll be able to find. Turkish coffee is quite strong. It's boiled up three or more times in small, long-handled pots. When the coffee is served—grounds and all—let it sit a minute so that the grounds can settle to the bottom of the cup, and then sip only half the cup. You'll have to let the waiter know in advance whether or not you want your coffee sweetened, as the sugar and coffee are brewed together. Milk, sugar or cream aren't served with the coffee. Ask for:

Turkish coffee	قهوة تركى	'æhwæ torki

And according to how much sugar you want, say:

very sweet	سكر زيادة	sokkar ziyædæ
medium	مضبوط	mazbūt
without sugar	سادة	sædæ

That's the end of our Arabic menu. For wine and other drinks, see the following pages. But after the feast comes…

The bill (check)

May I have the bill (check), please?	أريد الحساب من فضلك .	orīd æl ḥisæb min fadlak
Haven't you made a mistake?	ألا توجد غلطة ؟	'ælæ tūgæd galta
Is service included?	هل هذا يشمل الخدمة ؟	hæl hæzæ yæshmæl æl khidmæ
Is everything included?	هل هذا يشمل كل شيء ؟	hæl hæzæ yæshmæl koll shē'
Do you accept traveller's cheques?	هل تقبل الشيكات السياحية ؟	hæl takbæl æl shēkæt æl siyæḥiyyæ
Thank you, this is for you.	شكرا ، هذا لك .	shokran hæzæ læk
Keep the change.	احتفظ بالباقى .	'iḥtafiz bil bāki

That was a very good meal. We enjoyed it. Thank you.	كان الأكل عظيماً وأعجبنا جداً . شكراً .	kǣnæl 'ækl azīm wæ ææɡæbænǣ giddæn shokran
We'll come again sometime.	سنأتي مرة ثانية ان شاء الله .	sænæ'ti marra tænyæ 'in shǣ'allāh

الخدمة محسوبة
SERVICE INCLUDED

Complaints

But perhaps you'll have something to complain about...

That's not what I ordered. I asked for...	هذا ليس ما طلبته . أنا طلبت ...	hǣzæ læysæ mǣ talabto. 'ænǣ talabt
I don't like this/ I can't eat this.	هذا لا يعجبني / لا يمكن أن آكل هذا .	hǣzæ lǣ yo'giboni/læ yomkin 'æn 'ǣkol hǣzæ
May I change this?	هل يمكن تغيير هذا ؟	hæl yomkin tægyīr hǣzæ
The meat is...	اللحم ...	æl læḥm
overdone	شديد السواء	shædīd æl siwæ
underdone	قليل السواء	kalīl æl siwæ
too tough	ناشف جداً	nǣshif giddæn
This is too...	هذا ... جداً .	hǣzæ... giddæn
bitter/salty/sweet	مرّ / مالح / مسكر	morr/mǣliḥ/misakkar
The food is cold.	الأكل بارد .	æl 'ækl bǣrid
This isn't fresh.	هذا ليس طازة .	hǣzæ læysæ tāza
Would you ask the head waiter to come over?	اطلب من المتر الحضور من فضلك .	otlob minæl mitr æl ḥodūr min fadlak

Drinks

Beer

Beer has been drunk in the Middle East as far back as the ancient Egyptians and Mesopotamians. Good beer is still brewed in the Middle East, and today in Egypt you can ask for Stella beer (**bi**ræ **still**æ), a light, lager beer, or an Aswan beer (**bi**rit as**wān**), a dark beer; Almaza (al**ma**za) and Laziza (la**zi**za) are noted brands in Lebanon.

Wine

The Middle East was doubtless the birthplace of wine. From biblical times to the eighth century A.D., vineyards flourished. But Islam forbids the drinking of wine, and production was sharply curtailed. In the last century, however, wine production was stepped up considerably.

The wine cellars of Ksara in Lebanon, founded by the Jesuits in 1857, are the largest in the Middle East. Egypt's Gianaclis vineyards on the Nile Delta at Abu Hummus are noted. Most of the wine is white but among the red is the remarkable Omar Khayyam which is full-bodied and has a curious aftertaste of dates.

You'll only be able to order wine in large restaurants, especially those specializing in foreign dishes catering to foreign clientele.

Omar Khayyam (red)	عمر خيـام	omar khæy**yǣm**
Ptolemy (white)	نبيذ البطـالسة	ni**bīt** æl ba**tal**sæ
Matameer (red)	نبيذ المطامير	ni**bīt** æl mata**mīr**
Gianaclis (red or white)	نبيذ جناكليس	ni**bīt** zhænæ**klīs**
Queen Cleopatra (white)	نبيذ كليوباترة	ni**bīt** kilyo**ba**tra
Pharaoh's Wine (red)	نبيذ الفراعنة	ni**bit** æl **fara**'na

I'd like ... of wine.	أريد ... نبيذ .	orīd ... nibīt
a bottle	زجاجة	zogǣgit
half a bottle	نصف زجاجة	nisf zogǣgit
a glass	كبـاية	kobbæyit
I'd like something...	أريد شيئاً ...	orīd shæy'æn
sweet/sparkling/dry	حلوا/ بغازات/ جافا	ḥilw/bigǣzǣt/gǣf
I want a bottle of white wine.	أريد زجاجة نبيذ أبيض.	orīd zogǣgit nibīt 'abyad

red	أحمر	'aḥmar
white	أبيض	'abyad
rosé	روزيه	rozē

I don't want anything too sweet.	لا أريد شيئاً حلواً جداً .	lǣ orīd shē' ḥilw giddæn
How much is a bottle of...?	بكم زجاجة ... ؟	bikæm zogǣgit
Haven't you anything cheaper?	هل عندك شيء أرخص ؟	hæl 'ændæk shē' arkhas
Fine, that'll do.	هذا حسن .	hǣzæ ḥæsæn

If you enjoyed the wine, you may want to say:

Bring me another... please.	أريد ... آخر من فضلك .	orīd ... 'ākhar min fadlak
glass/bottle	كوب / زجاجة	kūb/zogǣgæ
What's the name of this wine?	ما اسم هذا النبيذ ؟	mǣ 'ism hǣzæ æl nibīt
Where does this wine come from?	من أين ياتى هذا النبيذ ؟	min 'æynæ yæ'ti hǣzæ æl nibīt
How old is this wine?	ما عمر هذا النبيذ ؟	mǣ 'omr hǣzæ æl nibīt

Other beverages

If you want some bottled mineral water, ask for *Sehha,* a mineral water from Lebanon.

I'd like some mineral water/a bottle of *Sehha.*	أريد ميـاه معدنية / زجاجة صحة .	orid miyǣh mæ'dæniyyæ/ zogǣgit siḥḥa

With the great abundance of fruit available, fruit juice is a very popular drink in the Arab countries. Don't miss the opportunity to stop at one of the stands selling fruit juice which will be freshly squeezed for you. Lemon, sugar-cane and mango juice are the favourites.

I'd like a/an ... juice.	أريد عصير ...	orid asir
apricot	مشمش	mishmish
carrot	جــزر	gazar
grape	عنب	'inæb
guava	جوافــة	gæwǣfæ
lemon	ليمون [حامض]	læmūn [ḥāmid]
mango	مــانجو	mængæ
orange	برتقــال	borto'ǣn
pomegranate	رمــان	rommān
strawberry	فراولــة	frawla
sugar-cane	قصب سكر	'asab sokkar
tamarind	تمر هنــدى	tamr hindi

A popular figure in Egypt is the *erkesoos* vendor, who walks the streets dressed in a colourful costume, calling attention to his presence by playing a type of finger bell. He'll gladly sell you a glass of *erkesoos* (a soft drink made from licorice) from the large bottle he carries. Just stop him and say:

I'd like a glass of *erkesoos,* please.	أريد كبــاية عرقسوس من فضلك .	orid kobbǣyit 'irkisūs min fadlak

Coffee house

Going to a café in an Arab country is more than just for refreshment. It's a tradition. Inside or on the terrace, observing the drama of Arab street life, the atmosphere of the café is one of calm and cordiality.

While you can also order tea, soft drinks or mineral water, you'll undoubtedly want to try Turkish coffee. You've a choice: you can order it without sugar, sweet or very sweet.

Two other important activities in a café are smoking a water pipe or nargile and playing backgammon and dominoes. If you decide to try the water pipe, clap your hands to attract the waiter's attention, and ask him for a *nargile*. You'll have to tell him whether you want *tamback,* a natural coarse-cut tobacco, or *ma assil,* a lighter tobacco mixed with molasses.

The waiter will prepare the pipe and the tobacco, take the first puff to see that it's well lit, and then turn it over to you.

It's likely that a shoe-shine boy will offer to shine your shoes if you're a man but he won't do it for women!

When you're ready to leave, clap your hands and ask the waiter for the bill. For tipping, see inside back-cover.

I'd like a cup of...	أريد فنجان . . .	orīd fingǣn
coffee	قهوة	'æhwæ
tea	شاى	shǣy
mint tea	شاى بنعناع	shǣy bini'nǣæ
I'd like a water pipe.	أريد شيشة [أرجيلة] .	orīd shīshæ ['argīlæ]
Bring us a backgammon board/some dominoes, please.	نريد طاولة / دومينو من فضلك .	norīd tawla/domino min fadlak

FOR COFFEE, see also page 58

Eating light—Snacks

Stopping for a snack is a very popular thing to do in Arab countries, especially since their equivalent to our snackbars are open nearly all night. So, after the cinema, a football game or a concert, you can stop at a snack-bar to sample *fool, falafel* or *shawerma*.

Give me two of these and one of those.	اعطيني ٢ من هذه و ١ من هذه .	'aatini 'itnēn min hæzihi wæ wǣḥid min hǣzihi
to the left/to the right	الى الشمال / الى اليمين	'ilæ æshshimǣl/'ilæl yæmīn
above/below	الى أعلى / الى أسفل	'ilæ 'æælæ/'ilæ 'æsfæl
I'd like a/an/some..., please.	أريد ... من فضلك .	orīd... min fadlak
cheese sandwich	سندوتش جبنة	sændæwitsh gibnæ
liver sandwich	سندوتش كبدة	sændæwitsh kibdæ
sausage sandwich	سندوتش سجق [معانق]	sændæwitsh sogo' [mæ'ǣnik]
roast beef sandwich	سندوتش روسبيف	sændæwitsh rozbīf
tongue sandwich	سندوتش لسان	sændæwitsh lisǣn
chicken sandwich	سندوتش فراخ	sændæwitsh firǣkh
baked macaroni, served with white sauce	مكرونة بالفرن	makarōna bil forn
bread	خبز	khobz
butter	زبدة	zibdæ
cake	كيك	kēk
hamburger	همبرجر	hamborgar
ice-cream	أيس كريم	'ǣys krīm
pastry	حلويات	ḥælæwiyyǣt
salad	صلاطة	salata
How much is that?	بكم هذا ؟	bikæm hǣzæ

Travelling around

The principal cities of Egypt—Cairo, Alexandria, Luxor and Aswan—are linked by regular flights. Because of their small area, Lebanon and Jordan aren't served by any domestic flights. At any airport you're sure to find someone who speaks English.

Do you speak English?	هل تتكلم الانجليزية ؟	hæl tætæ**kæ**llam ingilīzi
Is there a flight to Amman?	هل توجد رحلة الى عمان ؟	hæl **tū**gæd **riḥ**læ ilǣ 'æmmǣn
When's the next plane to Cairo?	ما موعد الطائرة القادمة الى القاهرة ؟	mǣ **mæw**'id æl tā'ira æl kādimæ ilǣ ælkāhira
Can I make a connection to Beirut?	هل أستطيع أن أعمل امتداد الى بيروت ؟	hæl astatī æn æ'mil 'imti**dǣd** ilǣ **bæy**rūt
I'd like a ticket to Damascus.	أريد تذكرة لدمشق .	orīd tæzkara li di**mishk**
What's the fare to Luxor?	ما الثمن الى الأقصر ؟	mǣ æl **tæ**mæn ilǣ **lok**sor
single (one-way)	ذهاب	zi**hǣb**
return (roundtrip)	ذهاب واياب	zi**hǣb** wæ 'i**yǣb**
What time does the plane take off?	متى تقوم الطائرة ؟	mætǣ tæ**kūm** æl tā'ira
What time do I have to check in?	متى يجب أن أقدم نفسى فى المطار ؟	mætǣ yægib æn o**kad**dim næfsi fil matār
What's the flight number?	ما نمرة الرحلة ؟	mǣ **nim**rit æl **riḥ**læ
What time do we arrive?	متى نصل ؟	mætǣ **na**sill

وصول ARRIVAL	رحيل DEPARTURE

Bus

Buses and taxis are the most important means of transportation in the Middle East. City buses provide a regular, if crowded, service. Cities are linked by ordinary and express services. Express buses are comfortable and very reasonably priced.

It isn't advisable to travel by bus in the big cities during the rush hours: buses are so overcrowded that you would have to hang on to the outside! If you are in Lebanon it might be better to try a collective taxi (called a *service*—særvis—in Arabic). A *service* will wait until it's full, and will then follow the regular bus route. These collective taxis operate in all major cities. Only slightly more expensive than the bus, they are often more convenient.

In Egypt collective taxis ply between Cairo and Alexandria. They leave from the railway station.

City buses show their destinations in Arabic and their route numbers in our figures. When you plan to take a bus the best thing is to ask your hotel desk clerk for directions.

City buses don't follow any set schedule. Buses run frequently, so just go to the bus stop and wait. Your bus is bound to come along soon. Interurban buses, on the other hand, do have time-tables.

Inquiries

I'd like a bus pass.	أريد اشتراك أوتوبيس .	**orīd ishtirāk otobīs**
Where can I get a bus/a collective taxi to...?	أين أجد أوتوبيس / تاكسى مشترك الى ... ؟	aynæ 'ægid otobīs/tæksi moshtarak 'ilæ
What bus do I take to Abou-Kir?	أى أوتوبيس أركب الى أبى قير ؟	æyy otobīs ærkæb ilæ 'æbūkīr

FOR TAXI, see page 27

What number is it to...?	ما النمرة للذهاب الى ...؟	mǣ æl **nimræ** lil **zihǣb ilǣ**
Where's the...?	أين ... ؟	æynæ
bus station	موقف الأوتوبيس	**maw**kif æl 'oto**bīs**
bus stop	محطة الأوتوبيس	ma**ḥat**tit æl 'oto**bis**
When's the ... bus to Amman?	متى يقوم الأوتوبيس ... الى عمان ؟	**mætǣ yakūm** æl 'oto**bīs**... ilǣ **'æm**mǣn
first/last/next	الأول / الأخير / القادم	æl **'æw**wæl/æl 'æ**khīr**/æl **kā**dim
Do I have to change buses?	هل يجب أن أغير الأوتوبيس ؟	hæl **yæ**gib æn o**gæy**yir æl 'oto**bis**
How long does the journey take?	ما مدة الرحلة ؟	mæ **mod**dit æl **riḥ**læ

Tickets

Where's the information office?	أين مكتب الاستعلامات ؟	æynæ **mæk**tæb æl '**is**ti'læmǣt
Where can I buy a ticket?	أين أشترى التذكرة ؟	**æy**næ æsh**tæ**ri æl taz**ka**ra
I want a ticket to Cairo.	أريد تذكرة للقاهرة .	o**rīd** taz**ka**ra lil **kā**hira
I'd like 2 singles to El Mansura.*	أريد تذكرتين ذهاب للمنصورة .	o**rīd** tazkar**tēn** zi**hæb** lil man**sū**ra
How much is the fare to Alexandria?	بكم التذكرة للاسكندرية ؟	bi**kæm** æl **taz**kara lil 'æskændæ**riy**yæ
Is it half price for a child? He's/She's 13.	هل أدفع نصف تذكرة للطفل ؟ سنه/سنها ١٣سنة.	hæl **æd**fæ' nisf taz**ka**ra lil tifl? **sin**no/sin**næ**hæ 13 **sæ**næ

Note: Children up to the age of five travel free.

* see grammar

FOR NUMBERS, see page 175

ذهاب أم ذهاب واياب ؟	Single or return (one-way or roundtrip)?
تدفع نصف تذكرة حتى سن . . .	It's half price up to the age of…
يجب أن تدفع تذكرة كاملة.	You'll have to pay full fare.

All aboard

Excuse me. May I get by?	آسف . أريد المرور .	ǣsif. orīd æl morūr
Is this seat taken?	هل هذا الكرسى محجوز ؟	hæl hǣzæl korsi mæḥgūz
Is this seat free?	هل هذا الكرسى فاضى ؟	hæl hǣzæl korsi fādi

ممنوع التدخين
NO SMOKING

I think that's my seat.	أظن أن هذا الكرسى لى .	azonn ænnæ hǣzæl korsi li
Can you tell me when we get to Memphis?	متى نصل الى ممفيس من فضلك ؟	mætǣ nasil ilǣ mæmfis min fadlak
What station is this?	ما هذه المحطة ؟	mǣ hǣzihi æl maḥatta
Will you tell me when to get off?	قل لى متى أنزل من فضلك .	'olli mætǣ ænzil min fadlak
I want to get off at Khan El-Khalili.	أريد النزول عند خان الخليلى .	orīd æl nozūl inda khǣn ælkhælili
Please let me off at the next stop.	من فضلك أنزلنى فى المحطة الجاية .	min fadlak ænzilni fil maḥatta æl gǣyyæ
May I have my luggage, please?	أريد شنطتى من فضلك .	orīd shantiti min fadlak

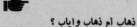

Train

What few passenger trains run in Jordan and Lebanon are slow and uncomfortable. Egypt, on the other hand, has a modern railway system with express trains. Fares are cheap, and trains are comfortable. During high season, it's advisable to reserve seats ahead of time.

Trains in Egypt generally have a dining-car, while sometimes hot meals can be served right at your seat. The steward will pass through the car to take your order. Usually, there's a set menu. You can also order drinks and sandwiches from him.

If you're in a hurry, take an air conditioned express train (with first and second class) which links major cities. For long trips, you can reserve a berth or compartment in a sleeping-car.

Children travel free up to the age of five and pay half-fare from six to ten. Note that at the railway station, ticket windows are segregated according to sex—and that the queue for women is generally shorter…

درجة أولى	FIRST CLASS
درجة ثانية	SECOND CLASS

To the station

Where's the railway station?	أين محطة السكة الحديد ؟	æynæ maḥattit æl **sikk**æ æl ḥædid
Taxi, please!	تاكسى !	**tæ**ksi
Take me to the railway station.	خذنى الى محطة السكة الحديد .	**khod**ni ilæ ma**ḥat**tit æl **sik**kæ æl ḥæ**did**

Inquiries

How much is the fare to Suez?	بكم التذكرة الى السويس ؟	bikæm æl tazkara ilǣ ælsiwēs
Is it a through train?	هل هو قطار مباشر ؟	hæl howæ kitār mobǣshir
Does the train stop at Al Minya?	هل يتوقف القطار فى المنيا ؟	hæl yætæwakkaf æl kitār fil minyæ
When is the ... train to Aswan?	متى يقوم القطار ... الى أسوان ؟	mætǣ yækūm æl kitār... ilǣ aswān
first/last/next	الأول / الأخير / القادم	æl 'æwwæl/æl 'ækhīr/æl kādim
What time does the train from Damascus arrive?	متى يصل القطار القادم من دمشق ؟	mætǣ yasil æl kitār æl kādim min dimishk
What time does the train for Alexandria leave?	متى يقوم قطار الاسكندرية؟	mætǣ yakūm kitār æl 'æskændæriyyæ
Is the train late?	هل القطار متأخر ؟	hæl æl kitār motæ'ækhkhir
Is there a dining-car/sleeping-car on the train?	هل توجد فى القطار عربة طعام / عربة نوم؟	hæl tūgæd fil kitār 'arabit ta'ām/'arabit nōm

دخول	ENTRANCE
خروج	EXIT
الى الرصيف	TO THE PLATFORMS

Platform (track)

What platform does the train for Suez leave from?	من أى رصيف يقوم قطار السويس ؟	min æyy rasīf yakūm kitār ælsiwēs
Where is platform 4?	أين رصيف ٤ ؟	æynæ rasīf 4
Is this the right platform for the train to Port-Saïd?	هل هذا هو الرصيف المضبوط لقطار بور سعيد ؟	hæl hǣzæ howæ æl rasīf æl mazbūt likitār bōr sa'īd

FOR TAXI, see page 27

انه قطار مباشر .	It's a direct train.
يجب أن تغير فى ...	You have to change at...
درجة أولى أم ثانية ؟	First or second class?
رصيف ... موجود ...	Platform ... is ...
هناك / تحت	over there/downstairs
على الشمال / على اليمين	on the left/on the right
قطار ... يقوم الساعة ... على رصيف ...	The train to ... will leave at ... from platform ...

Where's the ... ?

Where's the...?	أين ... ؟	æynæ
left luggage office	مكتب الأمانات	**mæk**tæb æl 'æmæ**nǣt**
lost property (lost and found) office	مكتب المفقودات	**mæk**tæb æl **mæf**kūdæt
newsstand	كشك الجرائد	koshk æl gar**ā**'id
restaurant	مطعم	**mat**'am
ticket office	شباك التذاكر	shib**bǣk** æl tæ**zǣ**kir
waiting room	صالة الانتظار	**sā**lit æl in**tizār**

Boat

Boats and steamers ply up and down the Nile. A trip on one of these magnificent, luxury steamers is well worthwhile. These boats are very chic and comfortable. You can take a relaxing one- or two-week cruise on one of them. From Cairo to Luxor takes about two weeks while the voyage from Aswan to Luxor or vice-versa lasts about a week.

The steamers put in at several ports, affording the opportunity to make land excursions. Tickets sold through travel

FOR TICKETS, see page 67

agents include full board on the ship plus an air ticket from Cairo to Aswan or Luxor. Local travel agents will advise you about sailing dates, which are usually once weekly or every two weeks.

There's also a one-day excursion by hydrofoil from Aswan to the ancient temple of Abu-Simbel with its enormous statue of Ramses II. Enquire about it at your hotel or travel agent's. In Cairo you can take a water-bus which you'll find quite pleasant.

When's the next steamer sailing for Luxor?	متى تقوم الباخرة القادمة الى الأقصر ؟	mætātækūmælbākhiraæl kādimæ ilā loksor
I'd like to book passage for 2 to Aswan.*	أريد أن أحجز تذكرتين لأسوان .	orīd æn æḥgiz tæzkartēn li'aswān
I want a return (roundtrip) ticket on the hydrofoil to the Abu-Simbel temple.	أريد تذكرة ذهاب وإياب الى معبد أبو سمبل على الهيدروفيل .	orīd tazkara zihāb wæ 'iyāb ilā mææbæd abūsimbil ælæl hidrōfīl

Other means of transportation

bicycle	عجلة [بسيكليت]	ægælæ [bisiklēt]
camelback riding	ركوب الجمل	rokūb æl gæmæl
helicopter	هليكوبتر	hilikobtar
hitchhiking	أوتوستوب	otostop
horseback riding	ركوب الخيل	rokūb æl khēl
moped (motorbike)	دراجة بخارية	darrāgæ bokhāriyyæ
motorcycle	موتوسيكل	motosikl

And if you're really stuck, start…

walking	امشى	'imshi

* see grammar

TRAVELLING AROUND

Around and about—Sightseeing

Here we're more concerned with the cultural aspect of life than with entertainment; and, for the moment, with towns rather than the countryside.

Can you recommend a good guide book on…?	من فضلك انصحنى بدليل سياحى جيد عن ...	min **fad**lak in**saḥ**ni bidæ**līl** siy**ǣ**ḥi gæy**yid** 'æn
Where's the tourist office?	أين مكتب السياحة ؟	æynæ **mæk**tæb æl siy**ǣ**ḥæ
What are the main points of interest?	ما أهم المعالم السياحية ؟	mǣ 'æ**hæm** æl mæ'**ǣ**lim æl siyæ**ḥī**yyæ
We're here for…	سنبقى هنا ..	sæ**nab**kā hon**ǣ**
only a few hours	بضعة ساعات فقط	**bid**'at sǣ'**ǣt** **fa**kat
a day	يوم	yōm
3 days	٣ أيام	3 æyy**ǣm**
a week	أسبوع	**os**bū
Can you recommend a (city) sightseeing tour?	من فضلك انصحنى بجولة سياحية (للمدينة) .	min **fad**lak in**saḥ**ni bi**gæw**læ siyǣ**ḥiy**yæ (lilmæ**dī**næ)
Where does the bus start from?	من أين يبدأ الأوتوبيس ؟	min æynæ **yæb**dæ' æl 'oto**bīs**
Will it pick us up at the hotel?	هل سيأخذنا من الفندق ؟	hæl sæyæ'**khoz**nǣ min æl **fon**dok
What bus/tram (street-car) should we take?	ما الأوتوبيس / الترام الذى نركبه ؟	mǣ æl 'oto**bīs**/æl ti**rām** ællæzi nær**kabo**
How much does the tour cost?	ما ثمن الجولة ؟	mǣ **tæ**mæn æl **gæw**læ
What time does the tour start?	متى تبدأ الجولة ؟	mæ**tǣ** **tæb**dæ' æl **gæw**læ
We'd like to rent a car for the day.	نريد تأجير سيارة ليوم .	no**rīd** tæ'**gīr** say**yā**ra li**yōm**
Is there an English-speaking guide?	هل يوجد مرشد سياحى يتكلم الانجليزية ؟	hæl **yū**gæd **mor**shid siy**ǣ**ḥi yætæ**kæl**læm æl 'ingiliziyyæ

FOR TIME OF DAY, see page 178

Where is/Where are the...?	أين ... ؟	æynæ
abbey	الدير	æl dēr
amusement park	مدينة الملاهى	mædīnæt æl mælæhi
aquarium	حديقة الأسماك	ḥædīkat æl 'æsmæk
art gallery	قاعة الفنون	kā'æt æl fonūn
artists' quarter	حى الفنانين	ḥæyy æl fænnænīn
bazaar	السوق [البازار]	æl sūk [æl bazār]
beach	الشاطىء	æl shāti'
botanical gardens	الحديقة النباتية	æl ḥædīka æl næbættiyyæ
bridge	الكوبرى [الجسر]	æl kobri [æl zhisr]
building	المبنى	æl mæbnæ
business district	حى الأعمال	ḥæyy æl 'æamæl
basilica	البازيليك	æl bæzilīk
castle	القصر	æl kasr
catacombs	سراديب الأموات	særædīb æl mæwtæ
cathedral	الكاتدرائية	æl kætidrā'iyyæ
citadel	القلعة	æl kalaa
city centre	وسط المدينة	wasat æl mædīnæ
city hall	مبنى المحافظة	mæbnæ æl moḥāfza
church	الكنيسة	æl kænīsæ
concert hall	قاعة الموسيقى	ka'æt æl mosīka
convent	الدير	æl dēr
docks	أرصفة الميناء	arsifat æl mīnæ
downtown area	وسط المدينة	wasat æl mædīnæ
exhibition	المعرض	æl maarad
factory	المصنع	æl masnaa
fortress	الحصن	æl ḥisn
fountain	النافورة	æl nafūra
gardens	الحدائق	æl hædæ'ik
harbour	الميناء	æl mīnæ
lake	البحيرة	æl boḥæyra
library	المكتبة	æl mæktæbæ

FOR ASKING THE WAY, see page 143

SIGHTSEEING

market	السوق	æl sūk
monastery	الدير	æl dēr
monument	النصب التذكارى	æl nasb æl tiz**kǣ**ri
mosque	الجامع	æl **gǣ**mi'
museum	المتحف	æl **mæ**tḥæf
observatory	المرصد	æl **mar**sad
old city	المدينة القديمة	æl mæ**dī**næ æl ka**dī**mæ
opera house	دار الأوبرا	dār æl **o**birā
palace	القصر	æl kasr
park	الحديقة	æl ḥæ**dī**ka
parliament building	مبنى البرلمان	**mæb**næ æl barla**mān**
presidential palace	القصر الجمهورى	æl kasr æl gum**hū**ri
pyramids	الأهرام	æl **ah**rām
river	النهر	æl nahr
royal palace	القصر الملكى	æl kasr æl **mæ**læki
ruins	الأطلال	æl **at**lāl
seafront	شاطىء البحر	shāti' æl baḥr
shopping centre	المركز التجارى	æl **mær**kæz æl to**gǣ**ri
sphinx	أبو الهول	**abul** hōl
stadium	الأستاد	æl '**is**tæd
statue	التمثال	æl **tim**sæl
stock exchange	البورصة	æl **bor**sa
swimming pool	حمام السباحة [البسين]	hæm**mǣm** æl si**bǣ**ḥæ [pisīn]
synagogue	المعبد اليهودى	æl **mæ**æbæd æl yæ**hū**di
temple	المعبد	æl mææ**bæd**
theatre	المسرح	æl **mas**raḥ
tomb	القبر	æl kabr
tower	البرج	æl borg
university	الجامعة	æl **gæm**'æ
walls	سور المدينة	sūr æl mæ**dī**næ
zoo	حديقة الحيوان	ḥæ**dī**kat æl ḥæyæ**wǣn**

Admission

Is the ... open on Fridays/Sundays?	هل ال ... مفتوح يوم الجمعة / الأحد ؟	hæl æl...mæftūḥ yōm æl gomaa/æl 'æḥæd
When does it open?	متى يفتح ؟	mætǣ yæftæḥ
When does it close?	متى يغلق [يقفل] ؟	mætǣ yoglak
How much is the admission charge?	بكم الدخول ؟	bikæm æl dokhūl
Is there any reduction for students/children?	هل يوجد تخفيض للطلبة / للأطفال ؟	hæl yūgæd takhfīd liltalaba/lil'atfāl
Have you a guide book in English?	هل عندك دليل سياحى بالانجليزية ؟	hæl indæk dælīl siyǣḥi bil 'ingiliziyyæ
Can I buy a catalogue?	هل أستطيع أن أشترى كتالوج ؟	hæl astatī' æn æshtæri kætælōg
Do you have any postcards?	هل عندك كروت ؟	hæl indæk korūt
Is it all right to take pictures?	هل أستطيع التصوير ؟	hæl æstatī' æl taswīr

الدخول مجانى	ADMISSION FREE
ممنوع التصوير	NO CAMERAS ALLOWED

Who—What—When?

What's that building?	ما هذا المبنى ؟	mǣ hǣzǣ æl mæbnǣ
Who was the...?	من كان ...؟	mæn kǣn
architect	المهندس	æl mohændis
artist	الفنان	æl fænnǣn
painter	الرسام	æl ræssǣm
sculptor	النحات	æl næḥḥǣt

Who built it?	من بناه؟	mæn bæn**ǣh**
Who painted that picture?	من رسم هذه الصورة؟	mæn **ræsæm** hǣzihi æl **sūra**
When did he live?	متى عاش ؟	mætǣ ǣsh
When was it built?	متى تم البناء ؟	mætǣ **tæmmæ** æl bi**nǣ'**
Where's the house where ... lived?	أين المنزل الذى عاش فيه ... ؟	æynæ æl **mænzil** æl**læzi** ǣshæ fih
We're interested in...	نحن مهتمين بـ ...	næḥno mohtæm**mīn** bi
antiques	الأنتيكات	æl ænti**kæt**
archeology	الآثار	æl **āsār**
art	الفن	æl fæn
botany	النباتات	æl næbǣ**tǣt**
ceramics	الفخار	æl fokh**khār**
coins	العملات	æl 'oml**ǣt**
crafts	العمل اليدوى	æl 'æmæl æl **yæ**dæwī
fine arts	الفنون الجميلة	æl fo**nūn** æl gæ**mī**læ
folk art	الفنون الشعبية	æl fo**nūn** æl shæ'**biy**yæ
furniture	الفرش [الموبيليا]	æl **fæ**rsh [æl mo**bil**yæ]
geology	الجيولوجيا	æl zhiyolo**zhi**æ
hieroglyphics	الهيروغليفيات	æl hirogli**fiy**yǣt
history	التاريخ	æl tǣ**rīkh**
local crafts	الفنون المحلية	æl fo**nūn** æl mæḥæl**liy**yæ
medicine	الطب	æl tibb
music	الموسيقى	æl mū**sī**ka
painting	الرسم	æl ræsm
pottery	الخزف	æl **khæ**zæf
prehistory	ما قبل التاريخ	mǣ kabl æl tǣ**rīkh**
sculpture	النحت	æl næḥt
zoology	علم الحيوان	ilm æl ḥæyæ**wǣn**
Where's the ... department?	أين قسم ... ؟	æynæ kism

Just the adjective you've been looking for...

It's...	. . . هذا	hææzæ
amazing	مدهش	modhish
awful	مخيف	mokhīf
beautiful	جميل	gæmīl
excellent	ممتاز	momtææz
interesting	مهم	mohim
magnificent	عظيم	azīm
monumental	عظيم	azīm
sinister	مشئوم	mæsh'ūm
strange	غريب	gærīb
stupendous	هائـل	hææ'il
superb	بديع	bædi'
terrible	مخيف	mokhīf
terrifying	مفزع	mofzi'
tremendous	هائل	hææ'il

Religious services

Islam is the religion of 90 per cent of the population of the Middle East, although Lebanon is almost evenly divided between Moslems and Christians. Among the Christian denominations, the Coptic Church is the largest with over six million adherents. Eastern Orthodox and Uniate Catholic churches are also found throughout the area. Small Protestant and Jewish groups exist in many Arab cities.

The faith of nearly 700 million people, Islam is the youngest of the world's great religions. The Koran represents the written revelations of God to the prophet Mohammed, and many of its greatest precepts parallel those of the Bible. In fact, Islam acknowledges the validity of Christian and Jewish teachings.

Spread principally through North Africa, the Middle East and large parts of Asia, Islam is divided into two major bodies plus many sects. But among the basic practices which should be followed by all Moslems are prayer five times daily facing Mecca, fasting during the sacred month of Ramadan, almsgiving and at least one pilgrimage to Mecca during the lifetime of each Moslem. The Koran forbids eating pork, drinking alcohol and gambling, but just as in the Christian West, modern life is bringing about a more relaxed attitude towards the observance of these practices.

Mosques are always open to visitors, except during worship. Picture-taking is permitted. The floors of the mosques are covered with beautifully-woven prayer rugs. To avoid soiling them, visitors and worshippers alike must remove their shoes before entering. At large mosques, over-sized slippers are available to visitors. If you make use of them it's customary to give the attendant a small tip. Don't wear shorts, miniskirts or bare-shouldered blouses in the mosque, and remember not to walk in front of people who are in prayer.

Is there a/an... near here?	هل يوجد... قريب من هنا؟	hæl **yū**gæd ... ka**rīb** min ho**nǣ**
Catholic church	كنيسة كاثوليكية	ki**nī**sæ kætōlī**kiy**yæ
Orthodox church	كنيسة أورثودوكس	ki**nī**sæ ortodo**ksiy**yæ
Protestant church	كنيسة بروتستنت	ki**nī**sæ protis**tant**
mosque	جامع	**gǣ**mi'
synagogue	معبد يهودى	mæ**æbæd** yæ**hū**di
At what time are the services?	ما هى مواقيت الصلاة ؟	mǣ **hi**yæ mæwā**kīt** æl sa**lāh**

Relaxing

Cinema (movies)—Theatre

There are many open-air cinemas operating from June to September which have double- or triple-feature programmes after sundown. The conventional indoor cinema has a feature film preceded by a newsreel, a documentary and commercials.

In both Egypt and Lebanon, American and English films are very popular and are shown in their original versions. In Egypt, the first showing normally starts at 3.30 p.m. except on Sundays and Fridays when there's a matinee at 10.30 a.m.

Theatre curtain time is usually 9.30 p.m. Booking in advance is a must. You can find out what's on by consulting the newspapers or publications of the type "This Week in..."

A renowned marionette show performs at special theatres in Egypt to the delight of young and old alike.

Have you the most recent "This Week in..."?	هل عندك آخر عدد من الأسبوع فى ... ؟	hæl **æn**dæk **ǣ**khir **æ**dæd min æl 'os**bū** fi
What's on at the cinema tonight?	ما هى الأفلام مساء اليوم ؟	mǣ **hi**yæ æl 'æf**lǣm** mi**sǣ**' æl yōm
What's playing at the theatre?	ما هى المسرحيات ؟	mǣ **hi**yæ æl masraḥiy**yǣt**
What sort of play is it?	ما نوع المسرحية ؟	mǣ nō' æl masra**ḥiyya**
Who's it by?	من المؤلف ؟	mæn æl mo'**æl**lif
Where's that new film by ... playing?	أين يدور فيلم... الجديد ؟	**æy**næ yæ**dūr** film...æl gæ**dīd**

Can you recommend (a)...?	هل تنصحنى بـ . . . ؟	hæl tæn**sa**ḥni bi
good film	فيلم جيد	film gæy**yid**
comedy	كوميديا	komidyæ
drama	دراما	drāma
musical	أوبريت	obē**rēt**
revue	عرض فنى	ard **fæ**nni
thriller	فيلم بوليسى	film bolīsi
Western	فيلم رعاة البقر	film ro**ǣt** æl **ba**kar
I'd like to see a puppet show.	أريد أن أشاهد عرضاً للعرائس .	**orīd** æn o**shǣ**hid ard lil **ara'**is
What time does it begin?	متى يبدأ ؟	**mætǣ yæb**dæ'
What time does the show end?	متى ينتهى العرض ؟	**mæ**tǣ yæn**tæ**hi æl 'ard
What time does the first evening performance start?	متى تبدأ أول حفلة فى المساء ؟	**mætǣ tæb**dæ' **æw**wæl **ḥæ**flæ fil mæ**sǣ'**
Are there any tickets for tonight?	هل توجد تذاكر لليلة ؟	hæl **tū**gæd tæ**zǣ**kir lil **lē**læ
I want to reserve 2 tickets for the show on Saturday evening.*	أريد أن أحجز تذكرتين لحفلة يوم السبت مساء .	**orīd** æn **æḥ**giz tazkar**tēn** li**ḥæ**flit yōm æl sæbt mæ**sǣ**'æn
Can I have a ticket for the matinee on Tuesday?	أريد تذكرة للحفلة الماتينية يوم الثلاثاء .	**orīd** tazkara lil **ḥæ**flæ æl mætīnē yōm æl solæ**sǣ'**
I want a seat in the stalls (orchestra).	أريد مكاناً فى الصالة .	**orīd** mæ**kǣn** fil **sā**la
Not too far back.	ليس الى الوراء كثيراً .	læysæ ilǣ æl **warā'** kæsīran

* see grammar

Opera—Ballet—Concert

Don't miss the opportunity to attend Middle Eastern music and dancing performances. At Lebanon's Baalbek ruins, ballets and concerts are held in the temple of Bacchus where local and internationally known artists perform. Among sound-and-light shows, you'll not want to miss the impressive production given at the Pyramids and the Citadel in Cairo and in Karnak.

In Beirut and Cairo you can also go to recitals and symphony concerts performed by both local and visiting artists.

Where's the opera house?	أين دار الأوبرا ؟	æynæ dār æl 'obira
Where's the concert hall?	أين صالة الموسيقى ؟	æynæ sālit æl mūsika
What's on at the opera tonight?	ماذا فى الأوبرا مساء اليوم؟	mæzæ fi æl 'obira mæsæ' æl yōm
Who's singing?	من يغنى ؟	mæn yogænni
Who's dancing?	من يرقص ؟	mæn yærkos
What time does the programme start?	متى يبدأ البرنامج ؟	mætæ yæbdæ' æl birnæmig
What orchestra is playing?	ما الفرقة التى تعزف ؟	mæ æl firka æl læti tææzif
What are they playing?	ماذا يعزفون ؟	mæzæ yææzifūn
Who's the conductor?	من رئيس الفرقة ؟	mæn ra'īs æl firka

آسف لا توجد أية مقاعد .	I'm sorry, we're sold out.
لم يبق سوى بعض المقاعد فى البلكون .	There are only a few seats in the balcony (circle).
أريد أن أرى تذكرتك من فضلك .	May I see your ticket?

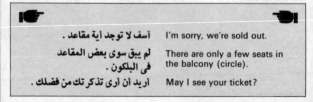

Night clubs

Night clubs are pretty much the same the world over, particularly when it comes to inflated prices. For most night clubs jacket and tie are sufficient.

In Beirut, the night clubs have a decidedly French flavour. If you only visit one night club during your visit, make sure the floor show features belly-dancers.

Can you recommend a good night club?	هل تنصحنى بملهى ليلى جيد ؟	hæl tan**saḥ**ni bi **mæl**hǣ **læy**li **gæy**yid
Is there a floor show?	هل يوجد عرض فنى ؟	hæl **yū**gæd 'ard **fæn**ni
Are there belly-dancers?	هل توجد راقصات شرقية ؟	hæl **tū**gæd rāki**sāt** shar**kiy**ya
What time does the floor show start?	متى يبدأ العرض الفنى ؟	**mæ**tǣ **yæb**dæ' æl 'ard æl **fæn**ni
Is evening dress necessary?	هل لبس السهرة ضرورى ؟	hæl libs æl **sah**ra da**rū**ri

And once inside ...

A table for 2, please.	ترابيزة [طاولة] لـ ٢ من فضلك .	tara**bē**zæ [**taw**la] li 2 min **fad**lak
My name's... I booked a table for 4.	اسمى ... لقد حجزت ترابيزة [طاولة] لـ ٤ .	**is**mi...**la**kad **ḥæ**gæzt tara**bē**za [**taw**la] li 4
We haven't got a reservation.	ليس عندنا حجز .	**læy**sæ in**dæ**nǣ **ḥægz**

FOR NUMBERS, see page 175

Dancing

Where can we go dancing?	أين يمكن الذهاب للرقص ؟	æynæ **yomkin** æl zih**ǣb** lil raks
Is there a discotheque anywhere here?	هل توجد مراقص هنا ؟	hæl **tū**gæd ma**rā**kis **honā**
There's a ball at the...	هناك حفلة فى ...	honāk **ḥæ**flæ fi
Would you like to dance?	هل ترقصين ؟	hæl tærko**sin**
May I have this dance?	هـل تسمحى لى بهذه الرقصة ؟	hæl tæs**ma**ḥi li bih**ǣ**zihi æl **rak**sa

Do you happen to play ... ?

On rainy days, this page may solve your problems.

Do you happen to play chess?	هل تلعب الشطرنج ؟	hæl tæl'**æb** shata**rang**
I'm afraid I don't.	آسف لا ألعب .	āsif lǣ **'æl**'æb
No, but I'll give you a game of back-gammon/domino.	لا . ولكنى أستطيع أن ألعب الطاولة / الدومينو	lǣ wæ læ**kin**ni asta**ti**' æn **'ǣl**'æb æl **taw**la/æl **do**mino
king	ملك	**mæ**lik
queen	وزير	wæ**zir**
castle (rook)	طابية	**tab**ya
bishop	فيـل	fil
knight	حصان [فرس]	ḥo**sān** [**fa**ras]
pawn	عسكرى [بيدق]	æs**kæ**ri [**bē**dæ']
Check mate!	كش مات !	kishsh **mǣt**
Do you play cards?	هل تلعب ورق [كوتشينة] ؟	hæl tæl'**æb wæ**ræk [kot**shī**næ]
ace	آس	**ǣs**
king	شايب [روا]	**shǣ**yib [**rwā**]
queen	بنت	bint
jack	ولد	**wæ**læd
joker	جوكر	**zhō**kar

spades	بستونى	bæstōni
hearts	كوبا	kobba
diamonds	دينارى	dinǣri
clubs	سباتى	sobǣti

Though gambling is forbidden by the Koran, casinos are operated all-year round in the Middle East for free-spending foreigners. To enter a casino, you must be over 21 and show your passport.

Oriental chess

In the Middle East, a very popular game is oriental chess, or backgammon, called *tawla* in Arabic. Shown below is the backgammon board. The game is played with dice. The winner is he who first has all his counters on his side.

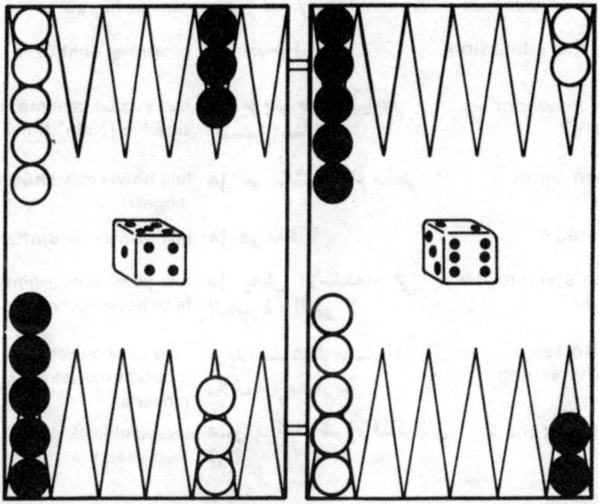

Sport

Football (soccer) is probably the favourite sport in the Middle East, especially in Egypt, but basketball, tennis and water sports are also very popular. Given the temperate-to-hot climate, water sports are practiced enthusiastically on the Mediterranean coastlines of Egypt and Lebanon and on the Nile. There is horse-racing on Saturdays and Sundays in Egypt.

Where's the nearest golf course?	أين أقرب ملعب جولف ؟	æynæ **ak**rab mæl'**æb** golf
Can we hire (rent) clubs?	هل يمكن تأجير العصيان ؟	hæl **yom**kin tæ'**gīr** æl 'os**yān**
Where are the tennis courts?	أين ملاعب التنس ؟	æynæ mæl**ǣ**'ib æl **ti**nis
Can I hire rackets?	هل يمكن تأجير المضارب ؟	hæl **yom**kin tæ'**gīr** æl ma**dā**rib
What's the charge per...?	ما الثمن لمدة ... ؟	mǣ æl **tæ**mæn li**mod**dæt
day/round/hour	يوم / لفة / ساعة	yōm/**læ**ffæ/**sǣ**'æ
What's the admission charge?	بكم الدخول ؟	bi**kæm** æl do**khūl**
Is there a swimming pool here?	هل يوجد حمام سباحة [بيسين] هنا ؟	hæl **yū**gæd ḥæm**mǣm** si**bǣ**ḥæ [pi**sin**] **ho**nǣ
Is it open-air or indoors?	هل هو مكشوف أم مغطى ؟	hæl **ho**wæ mæk**shūf** æm mo**gat**tā
Is it heated?	هل هو مدفأ ؟	hæl **ho**wæa mo**dæ**ffæ'
Can one swim in the lake/river?	هل يمكن الاستحمام فى البحيرة / النهر ؟	hæl **yom**kin æl 'istiḥ**mǣm** fil boḥæyra/æl nahr
I'd like to see a boxing/wrestling match.	أريد مشاهدة مباراة ملاكمة / مصارعة .	o**rīd** moshǣ**hæ**dæt mobā**rāt** mo**læk**mæ/ mo**sar**'a
Can you get me 2 tickets?*	هل يمكنك شراء تذكرتين لى ؟	hæl yom**ki**næk shi**rā'** tæzkar**tēn** li

* see grammar

Is there a football (soccer) match anywhere this Friday?	هل توجد مباراة كرة قدم يوم الجمعة ؟	hæl tūgæd mubarāt korit kadam yōm æl gomaa
Who's playing?	من يلعب ؟	mæn yæl'æb
Is there any good fishing around here?	هل الصيد جيد هنا ؟	hæl æl sēd gæyyid honæ
Do I need a permit?	هل أنا محتاج لترخيص ؟	hæl ænæ moḥtæg litarkhis
Where can I get one?	أين يمكن الحصول على ترخيص ؟	æynæ yomkin æl ḥosūl ælæ tarkhis
Is there a bowling alley/billiard hall near here?	هل يوجد ملعب بولنج / بلياردو قريب ؟	hæl yūgæd mæl'æb bōling/ bilyardo karīb

On the beach

Where's the beach?	أين الشاطىء ؟	æynæ æl shāti'
Is it safe for swimming?	هل الاستحمام أمان ؟	hæl æl 'istiḥmæm 'æmæn
Is there a lifeguard?	هل يوجد غطاس ؟	hæl yūgæd gattās
Is it safe for children?	هل هو أمان للأطفال ؟	hæl howæ 'æmān lil'atfāl
It's very calm.	انه هادىء جداً .	innæho hædi' giddæn
Is it a good place for snorkelling?	هل هو مكان مناسب للغطس ؟	hæl howæ mækæn monæsib lil gats
Are there dangerous currents?	هل توجد تيارات خطيرة ؟	hæl tūgæd tayyārāt khatīra
What time is high/ low tide?	متى المد / الجزر ؟	mætæ æl mædd/æl gæzr
What's the temperature of the water?	ما درجة حرارة المياه ؟	mæ daragit ḥarārit æl miyæh
I want to hire a/an/ some...	أريد تأجير ...	orīd tæ'gīr
air mattress	مرتبة هواء	mærtæbit hæwæ'
bathing hut	كابينة لخلع الملابس	kabīnæ likhæl'il mælæbis
bathing suit	مايوه	mæyō

deck chair	كرسى بلاج قماش	korsi plæzh 'omǣsh
skin-diving equipment	أدوات غطس	ædæwǣt gats
sunshade	شمسية	shæmsiyyæ
swimming belt	حزام نجاة [عوامة]	ḥizǣm nægǣ (æwwǣmæ)
tent	خيمة	khēmæ
water skis	أدوات انزلاق على الماء	ædæwǣt inzilǣk 'ælǣ æl mǣ'
Where can I rent a...?	أين أستأجر ... ؟	æynæ æstæ'gir
canoe	مركب	mærkib
motor boat	مركب بموتور [لنش]	mærkib bimotōr [lænsh]
rowing boat	مركب بمقاديف	mærkib bi mæ'ǣdīf
sailing boat	مركب شراعية	mærkib shira'iyyæ
What's the charge per hour?	بكم الساعة ؟	bikæm æl sǣ'æ

شاطىء خاص	ممنوع الاستحمام
PRIVATE BEACH	NO BATHING

Winter sports

From about mid-December until about mid-May you can ski at several locations in Lebanon.

I want to hire a/some...	أريد استئجار ...	orīd isti'gār
ski boots	بوط سكى	bōt ski
ski poles	عصى سكى	asā ski
skiing equipment	معدات سكى	mo'iddǣt ski
skis	سكى	skī
toboggan	زحليقة	zoḥlē'æ

Camping—Countryside

A sunny climate makes camping possible all year round—particularly along the Mediterranean Coast. However, campsites and facilities are limited, so check with the tourist office before setting out on your own. You can also camp near a house or on private land, but get permission from the owner first. People will always be happy to help you, and if you're lucky they'll even invite you in to share their meal.

Can we camp here?	هل نستطيع أن نعسكر هنا ؟	hæl næstat**ī** æn no'æ**s**kir honǣ
Where can one camp for the night?	أين نستطيع أن نعسكر الليلة ؟	æynæ nastat**ī** æn no'æ**s**kir æl **lē**læ
Is there a camping site near here?	هل يوجد معسكر قريب من هنا ؟	hæl **yū**gæd mo'**as**kar kar**ī**b min **honǣ**
Is there drinking water?	هل توجد مياه للشرب ؟	hæl **tū**gæd miy**ǣh** lil shorb
Are there shopping facilities on the site?	هل يوجد دكان فى المعسكر ؟	hæl **yū**gæd dok**kǣn** fil mo'**as**kar
Are there showers/ toilets?	هل يوجد دش / حمام ؟	hæl **yū**gæd doshsh/ ḥæm**mǣm**
What's the charge per day...?	بكم الليلة ... ؟	bi**kæm** æl **lē**læ
per person	لشخص	li**shakhs**
for a car	لسيارة	lisæy**yā**ra
for a tent	لخيمة	li**khē**mæ
Is there a youth hostel anywhere near here?	هل يوجد بيت شباب قريب ؟	hæl **yū**gæd bēt shæ**bǣb** kar**ī**b
Do you know anyone who can put us up for the night?	هل تعرف أحدا يقبل أن يسكننا عنده الليلة ؟	hæl **taa**rif æ**ḥ**ædæn **yak**bæl æn yosæk**ki**nonæ in**d**æho æl **lē**læ

FOR CAMPING EQUIPMENT, see page 107

CAMPING

ممنوع التخييم

CAMPING PROHIBITED

How far is it to...?	ما هى المسافة الى ... ؟	mæ hiyæ æl mæsæfæ ilæ
How far is the next village?	ما هى المسافة الى القرية القادمة ؟	mæ hiyæ æl mæsæfæ ilæ æl karya æl kādimæ
Are we on the right road for...?	هل نحن على الطريق الصحيح الى ... ؟	hæl næḥno ælæ æl tarīk æl saḥīḥ ilæ
Where does this road lead to?	الى أين يؤدى هذا الطريق ؟	ilæ æynæ yo'æddi hæzæ æl tarīk
Can you show us on the map where we are?	أين نحن على الخريطة من فضلك ؟	æynæ næḥno ælæ æl kharīta min fadlak

Landmarks

airfield	مطار	matār
bridge	كوبرى [جسر]	kobri [zhisr]
building	مبنى	mæbnæ
canal	قناة	kanæ
castle	قصر	kasr
cliff	حافة الجبل	ḥæffit æl gæbæl
copse	أعشاب	ææshæb
crossroads	مفترق طرق [تقاطع]	moftarak torok [takāto]
desert	صحراء	saḥrā'
excavations	تنقيب عن الآثار	tankīb æn æl āsār
farm	عزبة	'izba
ferry	معدية	mi'æddiyyæ
field	حقل	ḥakl
footpath	سكة	sikkæ
hamlet	قرية	karya
hill	تل	tæll
house	بيت	bēt

CAMPING

inn	استراحة	istirāḥa
lake	بحيرة	boḥēra
mound	تـل	tæll
mountain	جبل	gæbæl
mountain range	سلسلة جبال	silsilit gibǣl
oasis	واحة	wǣḥæ
path	سكة	sikkæ
plain	سهل	sæhl
plantation	مزرعة	mazraa
pool	بركة	birkæ
railway	خط سكة حديد	khatt sikkæ ḥædīd
river	نهر	nahr
road	طريق	tarīk
ruins	أطلال	atlāl
sand dunes	تلال رملية	tilǣl ramliyyæ
sea	بحر	baḥr
spring	منبع	mænbææ
tower	برج	borg
track	سكة	sikkæ
tree	شجرة	shagara
valley	وادى	wǣdi
village	قرية	karya
wadi	وادى	wǣdi
well	بئر	bi'r
wood	غابة	gǣbæ
What's the name of this place?	ما اسم هذا المكان ؟	mǣ ism hǣzæ æl mækǣn
How high is that mountain?	ما ارتفاع هذا الجبل ؟	mǣ irtifǣ' hǣzæ æl gæbæl

Making friends

Introductions

Despite the language barrier, you'll have no problem in striking up a conversation with Arabs, especially when they realize that you're a foreigner. As a matter of fact, they'll probably start the conversation first. Arabs are eager to help foreigners, and they're curious to learn about your country and way of life. It's quite possible that a chance meeting with an Arab will soon lead to an invitation to meet his family at home. Do accept, as such spontaneous hospitality is sincere, and bring some sweets or flowers for the hostess.

Here are a few phrases to get you started.

How do you do? How are you?	ازيك [كيفك] ؟	izzæyyæk [kīfæk]
Very well, thank you.	بخير . الحمد لله .	bikhēr. ælḥæmdolillǣh
How's life?	كيف الحال ؟	kæyfæl ḥǣl
Fine thanks. And you?	كويس شكراً . وأنت ؟	kwæyyis shokran. wæ intæ
May I introduce Miss...	أقدم لك الآنسة ...	okaddim læk æl 'ǣnissæ
I'd like you to meet a friend of mine.	أحب أن تقابل صديقاً لى .	oḥib æn tokābil sadīkan lī
Ali, this is...	يا على ، هذا ...	yǣ ali hǣzæ
My name's...	اسمى ...	ismi
Glad to know you.	تشرفنا .	tæsharrafna

Follow-up

How long have you been here?	منذ متى وأنت هنا ؟	monzo mætǣ wæ intæ hobǣ
We've been here a week.	نحن هنا منذ أسبوع .	næḥno honǣ monzo osbū

Is this your first visit?	هل هذه أول زيارة لك ؟	hæl hǣzihi awwal ziyāra læk
No, we came here last year.	لا . أتينا السنة الماضية .	lǣ. ætæynæ æl sænæ æl mādiyæ
Are you enjoying your stay?	هل أنت مبسوط هنا ؟	hæl 'æntæ mabsūt honǣ
Yes. I like ... very much.	نعم . . . تعجبنى جداً .	næ'æm ... to'giboni giddæn
Are you on your own?	هل أنت وحدك ؟	hæl æntæ wæḥdæk
I'm with...	أنا مع ...	ænǣ mææ
my wife	زوجتى	zæwgæti
my husband	زوجى	zæwgi
my family	أسرتى	osrati
my parents	والداى	wǣlidǣy
some friends	أصحابى	'asḥābi
Where do you come from?	من أين تاتى ؟	min æynæ tæ'ti
What part of ... do you come from?	من أى مكان فى ... تاتى ؟	min ayy mækǣn fi ... tæ'ti
I'm from...	أنا من ...	ænǣ min
Where are you staying?	أين تسكن ؟	æynæ tæskon
I'm a student.	أنا طالب .	ænǣ tālib
What are you studying?	ماذا تدرس ؟	mǣzǣ tædross
We're here on holiday.	نحن هنا فى اجازة [فرصة] .	næḥno honǣ fi ægǣzæ [forsa]
I'm here on a business trip.	أنا هنا لشغل .	ænǣ honǣ li shogl
What kind of business are you in?	ما ذا تشتغل ؟	mǣzæ tæshtægil
I hope we'll see you again soon.	أرجو أن أراك مرة أخرى قريباً ان شاء الله .	argū æn arākæ marra okhrā karībæn 'in shǣ'allāh
See you later/See you tomorrow.	الى اللقاء / أراك غداً .	ilǣ æl likā'/arākæ gædæn

The weather

The Arabs don't talk about the weather as much as we do, but if you can't think of a better way to enter into conversation with someone, try…

What a lovely day!	انه يوم جميل .	innæho yōm gæ**mīl**
What awful weather!	الجو سيء [وحش] .	æl gæw **sæ**yyi' [wiḥish]
Isn't it hot/cold today?	أليس الجو حاراً / بارداً اليوم ؟	ælæysæ æl gæw ḥarr/bærd æl yōm
The wind is very strong.	الهواء شديد جداً .	æl hæ**wǣ'** shæ**dīd** **gid**dæn
What's the temperature outside?	ما درجة الحرارة بالخارج ؟	mǣ **da**ragit æl ḥa**rā**ra bil **khǣ**rig
What's the weather forecast?	ما هى التنبؤات الجوية ؟	mǣ hiyæ æl tænæbbo'**ǣt** æl gæw**wiy**yæ

Invitations

My wife and I would like you to dine with us on…	زوجتى وأنا نحب أن تتعشى معنا يوم …	zæw**gæ**ti wæ æ**nǣ** no**ḥibb** æn tætæ'**æsh**shǣ **mæ'**æ-næ yōm
Can you come to dinner tomorrow night?	هل تستطيع أن تاتى للعشاء مساء الغد ؟	hæl tasta**tī** æn **tæ'**ti lil æ**shǣ'** mæ**sǣ'** æl gædd
Can you join us for a drink this evening?	هل تشاركنا فى مشروب مساء اليوم ؟	hæl tu**shǣrik**næ fi mash**rūb** mæ**sǣ'** æl yōm
There's a party. Are you coming?	هناك حفلة هل تاتى ؟	ho**nǣk** **ḥæf**læ. hæl **tæ'**ti
That's very kind of you.	هذا لطيف جداً منك .	**hǣ**zæ la**tīf** **gid**dæn **min**kæ
Great, I'd love to come.	عظيم ، يسرنى أن أحضر .	a**zīm**. yæsor**ro**ni æn **aḥ**dar

FOR TEMPERATURE, see page 183

What time shall we come?	متى نأتى ؟	mætǣ næ'ti
May I bring a friend (male/female)?	هل يمكن أن يأتى صديقى / صديقتى ؟	hæl **yom**kin æn yæ'ti sa**dī**ki/sadi**ka**ti
I'm afraid we've got to go now.	نستأذن فى الرحيل .	næs**tæ**'zin fil ra**ḥīl**
Next time you must come to visit us.	المرة القادمة يجب أن تـأتى لزيارتنا .	æl **mar**ra æl **kā**dimæ **yæ**gib æn **tæ**'ti liziyā**ra**tinæ
Thank you very much for an enjoyable evening.	شكراً جزيلا على هذه السهرة الجميلة .	**sho**kran gæ**zī**læn 'ælæ **hæ**zihi æl **sah**ra æl gæ**mī**læ
Thanks for the party. It was great.	شكراً على الحفلة . كانت عظيمة .	**sho**kran 'ælǣ æl **ḥæf**læ. **kæ**næt a**zī**ma

Dating

Would you like a cigarette?	سيجارة ؟	si**gā**ra
Have you got a light, please?	أريد أن أولّـع من فضلك.	o**rīd** æn awæl**læ**æ min **fad**lak
Can I get you a drink?	هل أقدم لك كأساً ؟	hæl o**kad**dim **læ**ki **kæ**'sæn
Excuse me, could you please help me?	هل تساعدينى من فضلك ؟	hæl tosæ'i**dī**ni min **fad**lik
I'm lost. Can you show me the way to...?	أنا تائه . من فضلك أرشدينى الى . . .	æ**nǣ tǣ'ih**. min **fad**lik ærshi**dī**ni i**lǣ**
Are you waiting for someone?	هل تنتظرين أحداً ؟	hæl tantazi**rī**næ æ**ḥæ**dæn
Are you free this evening?	هل أنت فاضية مساء اليوم ؟	hæl **æn**ti **fad**yā mæ**sǣ**' æl yōm
Would you like to go out with me tonight?	هل تحبين الخروج معى الليلة ؟	hæl toḥib**bī**næ æl kho**rūg** **mæ**'i æl **lē**læ

Would you like to go dancing?	هل تحبين الذهاب للرقص ؟	hæl toḥibbīnæ æl zihææb lil raks
I know a good discotheque/restaurant.	أعرف مرقصا/مطعماً جيداً .	æærif markas/mat'am gæyyid
Shall we go to the cinema (movies)?	هل نذهب الى السينما ؟	hæl næzhæb ilææ æl sinimææ
I'd love to, thank you.	نعم أحب ، شكراً .	nææm oḥibb shokran
Where shall we meet?	أين نتقابل ؟	æynæ nætækābæl
When shall I pick you up?	فى أى ساعة أمر عليك للخروج ؟	fi æyy sææ'æ æmorr ælæyki lil khorūg
I'll call for you at 8.	سأحضر الساعة ٨ .	sæ'aḥdar æl sææ'æ 8
May I take you home?	هل أوصلك الى منزلك ؟	hæl awassalik ilææ mænzilik
Can I see you again tomorrow?	هل نتقابل غداً ؟	hæl nætækābæl gædæn
Thank you, it's been a wonderful evening.	شكراً . كانت سهرة ممتازة .	shokran. kæænæt sahra momtææzæ
I've enjoyed myself tremendously.	أنا انبسطت جداً .	'ænææ inbasatt giddæn
What's your telephone number?	ما نمرة تليفونك ؟	mææ nimrit tilifōnik
Do you live with your family?	هل تسكنين مع أسرتك ؟	hæl tæskonīnæ mæ'æ osratik
Do you live alone?	هل تسكنين وحدك ؟	hæl tæskonīnæ wæḥdik
What time do you have to be back?	متى يجب أن تعودى الى المنزل ؟	mætææ yægib 'æn tæ'ūdi ilææ æl mæænzil

Shopping guide

This shopping guide is designed to help you find what you want with ease, accuracy and speed. It features:

1. a list of all major shops, stores and services;
2. some general expressions required when shopping to allow you to be specific and selective;
3. full details of the shops and services most likely to concern you. Here you will find advice, alphabetical lists of items and conversion charts listed under the headings below.

Advice

In Egypt and Jordan, stores are open from 8.30 a.m. to 12.30 p.m. and from 4 to 7 p.m., Monday to Thursday, and from 8.30 a.m. to 12.30 p.m. on Saturdays. Although some small shops remain open on Friday, offices and department stores are closed. On Sunday the large stores are shut, but all other activities continue normally. In Lebanon, hours vary according to the season: from November to May stores are open from 8.30 a.m. to 1 p.m. and from 3 to 6 p.m., Monday to Friday, and from 8.30 a.m. until 12.30 p.m. on Saturdays. During the summer months they're open on weekdays from 8 a.m. until 1 p.m. only and are closed on Saturdays and Sundays.

Souk means "market" in Arabic. It's composed of a maze of narrow, winding alleys where all kinds of tradesmen and artisans are grouped together.

In the *souk* you'll see all sorts of jewellers and artisans at work inlaying wood with enamel and ivory, engraving or hammering copper or making pottery. Antique dealers abound, and merchants sell fine rugs and brocades—all this in an atmosphere scented with sandalwood, cinnamon and musk.

If you are interested in antiques, with a little luck you might come across an ancient coin, a piece of Coptic cloth or a statuette dating back to the pharaohs. Be sure to demand a museum certificate guaranteeing the authenticity of any very old objects you buy.

Remember that selling and bargaining are Eastern customs not without a certain charm. As you browse through the *souk,* take your time, and don't hesitate to accept a cup of coffee or mint tea offered you by a merchant.

Shops, stores and services

Where's the nearest...?	أين أقرب ... ؟	æynæ akrab
antique shop	محل أنتيكات	mæḥæll æntikæt
art gallery	معرض فنون	maarad fonūn
bakery	مخبز	mækhbæz
bank	بنك	bænk
barber's	حلاق	ḥællāk
bazaar	بازار [سوق]	bazār [sūk]
beauty salon	صالون تجميل	salōn tægmīl
bookshop	مكتبة	mæktæbæ
butcher	جزار [لحام]	gazzār [læḥḥæm]
candy store	محل حلويات [ملبِّس]	mæḥæll ḥælæwiyyæt [milæbbiss]
chemist's	أجزخانة [فرماشية]	ægzækhænæ [færmæshiyyæ]
clothing store	محل ملابس	mæḥæll mælæbis
cobbler	جزمجى [كندرجى]	gæzmægi [kindarzhi]
dairy	محل ألبان	mæḥill ælbæn
dentist	طبيب أسنان	tabib æsnæn
department store	محل كبير	mæḥæll kæbir
doctor	دكتور	doktōr
dressmaker	خياطة	khayyāta
drugstore	أجزخانة [فرماشية]	ægzækhænæ [færmæshiyyæ]
dry cleaner	محل تنظيف ملابس	mæḥæll tanzīf mælæbis
fishmonger	محل سمك	mæḥæll sæmækk
florist	محل زهور	mæḥæll zohūr
furrier	محل فرو	mæhæll farrw
greengrocer	خضرى	khodari
grocery	بقال	bakkāl
hairdresser's (ladies)	صالون تجميل	salōn tægmīl
hardware store	محل أدوات منزلية	mæḥæll ædæwæt mænziliyyæ
hat shop	محل برانيط	mæḥæll baranit

SHOPPING GUIDE

hospital	مستشفى	mostæshfæ
ironmonger	محل أدوات منزلية	mæḥæll ædæwǣt mænziliyyæ
jeweller	جواهرجى	gæwæhirgi
laundry	غسيل ومكوة	gæsīl wæ mækwæ
leather-goods store	محل مصنوعات جلدية	mæḥæll masnū'āt gildiyyæ
market	سوق	sūk
milliner	صانعة برانيط	sāni'æt baranīt
newsagent	بائع جرائد	bæ'i' garā'id
newsstand	كشك جرائد	koshk garā' id
optician	محل نظارات [عوينات]	mæḥæll nazzarāt [owæynǣt]
pastry shop	حلوانى	ḥælæwǣni
perfumery	محل عطور	mæḥæll otūr
photographer	مصور	mosawwir
photo shop	محل تصوير	mæḥæll taswīr
police station	قسم بوليس	kism bolīs
post office	مكتب بريد	mæktæb bærīd
shoemaker (repairs)	جزمجى [كندرجى]	gæzmægi [kindarzhi]
shoe shop	محل جزم [أحذية]	mæḥæll gizæm [æḥziyæ]
souvenir shop	محل سوفنير	mæḥæll sūvinīr
sporting goods shop	محل أدوات رياضية	mæḥæll ædæwǣt riyāddiyya
stationer	مكتبة	mæktæbæ
supermarket	سوبر ماركت	sūpir markit
sweet shop	محل حلويات [ملبس]	mæḥæll ḥælæwiyyǣt [milæbbis]
tailor	ترزى [خياط]	tærzi [khayyāt]
tobacconist	محل سجاير [دخان]	mæḥæll sægǣyir [dokhkhǣn]
travel agent	مكتب سياحى	mæktæb siyǣḥi
vegetable store	خضرى	khodari
veterinarian	طبيب بيطرى	tabīb bitari
watchmaker	محل ساعات	mæḥæll sæǣt

General expressions

Here are some expressions which will be useful to you when you're out shopping.

Where?

Where's a good…?	أين يوجد … جيد ؟	æynæ yūgæd…gæyyid
Where can I find a…?	أين أجد … ؟	æynæ ægid
Where do they sell…?	أين يباع … ؟	æynæ yobǣ'
Can you recommend an inexpensive…?	هل يمكنك أن تنصحنى بـ… رخيص ؟	hæl yomkinæk æn tænsaḥni bi…rakhīs
Where's the main shopping area?	أين مركز المحلات الرئيسى ؟	æynæ mærkæz æl mæḥillǣt æl ra'īssi
How far is it from here?	ما بعده عن هنا ؟	mǣ bo'doh æn honǣ
How do I get there?	كيف أصل اليه ؟	kæyfæ asil ilæyhi

Service

Can you help me?	هل يمكنك مساعدتى ؟	hæl yomkinæk mosæ'ædæti
I'm just looking around.	اننى أتفرج فقط .	innæni ætæfarrag fakatt
I want…	أريد . . .	orīd
Can you show me some…?	هل يمكنك أن ترينى … ؟	hæl yomkinæk æn torīni
Have you any…?	هل عندك … ؟	hæl indæk

That one

Can you show me that one?	من فضلك أرينى هذا .	min fadlak ærīni hǣzæ
It's over there.	انه هناك .	innæho honǣk

Defining the article

I want a ... one.	أريد شيئاً ...	orīd shæy'æn
big	كبير	kæbīr
coloured	ملون	molæwwæn
dark	غامق	gǣmik
good	جيد	gæyyid
heavy	ثقيل	ti'īl
large	كبير	kæbīr
light (weight)	خفيف	khæfīf
light (colour)	فاتح	fǣtiḥ
long	طويل	tawīl
round	مستدير	mostædīr
short	قصير	kasīr
small	صغير	sagīr
square	مربع	morabbaa
I don't want anything too expensive.	لا أريد شيئاً غاليا .	lǣ orīd shæy'æn gǣliyæn

Preference

Can you show me some more?	أريد أن أرى شيئاً آخراً من فضلك .	orīd æn arā shæy'æn ākhar min fadlak
Haven't you anything...?	هل عندك شيء ... ؟	hæl indæk shē'
cheaper/better	أرخص / أحسن	arkhas/æḥsæn
larger/smaller	أكبر / أصغر	akbar/asgar

How much?

How much is this?	بكم هذا ؟	bikæm hǣzæ
I don't understand. Please write it down.	لا أفهم . من فضلك أكتب لى الثمن.	lǣ æfhæm. min fadlak iktib li æl tæmæn
I don't want to spend more than...	لا أريد أن أدفع أكثر من ...	lǣ orīd æn ædfææ aktar min

FOR NUMBERS, see page 175

Decision

That's just what I want.	هذا هو المطلوب .	hæzæ howæl matlūb
No, I don't like it.	لا . لا تعجبنى .	læ. læ to'giboni
I'll take it.	سآخذها .	sæ'ækhodhæ

Ordering

Can you order it for me?	هـل يمكنك أن توصى عليها لى ؟	hæl yomkinæk æn towassi ælæyhæ li
How long will it take?	متى تكون جاهزة ؟	mætæ tækūn gæhizæ

Delivery

I'll take it with me.	سآخذها معى .	sæ'ækhodhæ mæ'i
Deliver it to the ... hotel.	وصلها الى فندق ...	wassilhæ ilæ fondok
Please send it to this address.	من فضلك أرسلها الى هذا العنوان .	min fadlak ærsilhæ ilæ hæzæl 'inwæn
Will I have any difficulty with the customs?	هل سأجد صعوبة فى الجمرك؟	hæl sæ'ægid so'ūba fil gomrok

Paying

How much is it?	بكم ؟	bikæm
Can I pay by traveller's cheque?	هل يمكن الدفع بشيكات سياحية ؟	hæl yomkin æl dæf' bishēkæt siyæḥiyyæ
Do you accept dollars/pounds/credit cards?	هل تقبـل الدولارات / الجنيهات / بطاقات الرصيد ؟	hæl takbal æl dōlārāt/æl gonæyhæt/bitākāt æl rasid
Haven't you made a mistake in the bill?	ألا توجد غلطة فى الفاتورة ؟	'ælæ tūgæd galta fil fatūra
Can I have a receipt, please?	أريد فاتورة [ايصال] من فضلك .	orid fatūra ['isāl] min fadlak

Anything else?

No, thanks, that's all.	لا ، شكراً . يكفي هذا .	**lææ shokran. yækfī hææzæ**
Yes, I want...	نعم ، أريد ...	**næ**æm. or**ī**d
Thank you. Good-bye.	شكراً . مع السلامة .	**shok**ran. maassæ**lææ**mæ

Dissatisfied

Can you please exchange this?	هل يمكنك تغيير هذا من فضلك ؟	hæl yom**ki**næk tæg**yīr** **hææ**zæ min **fad**lak
I want to return this.	أريد ارجاع هذا .	o**rīd** ir**gææ'** **hææ**zæ
I'd like a refund.	أريد استرداد الثمن .	o**rīd** istir**dææd** æl tæmæn
Here's the receipt.	هذا هو الايصال .	**hææ**zæ **ho**wæl 'i**sāl**

هل استطيع مساعدتك ؟	Can I help you?
أى ... تريد ؟	What ... would you like?
لون / شكل	colour/shape
نوع / كمية	quality/quantity
آسف . ليس عندى منه .	I'm sorry, we haven't any.
لقد انتهى ما كان عندنا منه.	We're out of stock.
هل نوصى لك عليه ؟	Shall we order it for you?
هل تاخذه معك أم يجب أن نرسله لك ؟	Will you take it with you or shall we send it?
أى شىء آخر ؟	Anything else?
... (الثمن) من فضلك .	That's ... please.
لا نقبل ...	We don't accept...
بطاقات الرصيد	credit cards
الشيكات السياحية	traveller's cheques
الشيكات الخاصة	personal cheques

Bookshop—Stationer's—Newsstand

In the Middle East, bookshops and stationers may be combined or separate. Newspapers and magazines may be sold in bookshops, in kiosks or at the stationer's.

Where's the nearest...?	أين أقرب ... ؟	æynæ akrab
bookshop	مكتبة	mæktæbæ
stationer's	محل أدوات كتابة	mæḥæll ædæwæt kitæbæ
newsstand	كشك جرائد	koshk garā'id
I want to buy a/an/some...	أريد شراء ...	orīd shirā'
address book	دفتر عناوين	daftar ænæwīn
ball-point pen	قلم حبر جاف	kalam ḥibr gæf
book	كتاب	kitæb
box of paints	علبة ألوان	ilbit ælwæn
carbon paper	ورق كربون	warak karbōn
cellophane tape	شريط لاصق	shirīt lāsik
crayons	أقلام ألوان	aklām ælwæn
dictionary	قاموس	kamūs
Arabic–English	عربى – انجليزى	arabi-ingilīzi
English–Arabic	انجليزى – عربى	ingilīsi-arabi
pocket dictionary	قاموس للجيب	kamūs lil gēb
drawing paper	ورق رسم	warak ræsm
drawing pins	دبابيس رسم	dæbæbis ræsm
envelopes	ظروف	zorūf
eraser	أستيكة [ممحاة]	æstīkæ [mimḥæh]
fountain pen	قلم حبر	kalam ḥibr
glue	صمغ	samg
grammar book	كتاب نحو	kitæb næḥw
guide book	دليل سياحى	dælīl siyæḥi
ink	حبر	ḥibr
black/red/blue	أسود/ أحمر/ أزرق	æswæd/aḥmar/æzrak

SHOPPING GUIDE

labels	بطاقات	bitākāt
magazine	مجلة	mægællæ
map	خريطة	kharīta
map of the town	خريطة للمدينة	kharīta lil mædīnæ
road map	خريطة للطرق	kharīta lil torok
newspaper	جريدة	gærīdæ
American/English	أمريكانى / انجليزى	æmrikǣni/ingilīzi
notebook	مفكرة [بلوك نوت]	mofækkira [blok-nōt]
note paper	ورق خطابات	warak khitabāt
paperback	كتاب جيب	kitǣb gēb
paper napkins	فوط ورق	fowatt warak
pen	قلم حبر	kalam ḥibr
pencil	قلم رصاص	kalam rosās
pencil sharpener	برّاية	bærrǣyæ
playing cards	ورق لعب [كوتشينة]	warak liib [kotshīnæ]
postcards	كروت بوستال	korūt postāl
refill (for a pen)	أنبوبة حبر جاف	onbūbit ḥibr gæf
rubber	أستيكة [ممحاة]	æstīkæ [mimḥæh]
rubber bands	أستيك	æstik
ruler	مسطرة	mastara
sketching block	كراس سكتش	korrās skitch
stamps	طوابع بريد	tawābi' bærīd
string	خيط [دوبار]	khēt [dobār]
thumb tacks	دبابيس رسم	dæbæbīs ræsm
tissue paper	ورق كلينكس	warak klīniks
typewriter ribbon	شريط لآلة كاتبة	shirīt li'ǣlæ kǣtbæ
typing paper	ورق لآلة كاتبة	warak li'ǣlæ kǣtbæ
wrapping paper	ورق لف	warak læff
writing pad	بلوك ورق	blok warak
Where's the guide-book section?	أين قسم «الدليل السياحى»؟	æynæ kism "æl dælīl æl siyǣhi"
Where do you keep the English books?	أين قسم الكتب الانجليزية ؟	æynæ kism æl kotob æl 'ingiliziyyæ

Camping

I'd like a/an/some...	أريد ...	orīd
axe	بالطة	balta
bottle-opener	فتاحة زجاجات	fættææḥit zogægææt
bucket	جردل [سطل]	gærdæl [satl]
butane gas	أنبوبة بوتاجاز	onbūbit botægææz
camp cot	سرير للسفر	sirir lil safar
camping equipment	معدات تخييم	mo'iddææt tækhyīm
can opener	فتاحة علب	fættææḥit 'ilæb
candles	شمع	shæm'
(folding) chair	كرسى (بلاج)	korsi (plæzh)
compass	برجل [بيكار]	bærgæl [bikār]
corkscrew	بِّريمة لفتح الزجاجات	bærrīmæ lifæth æl zogægææt
crockery	أطباق	atbāk
cutlery	فضية	faddiyyæ
first-aid kit	علبة اسعافات أولية	ilbitt is'ææfææt æwwæliyyæ
flashlight	بطــارية	battāriyyæ
frying pan	طاسة	tāsa
groundsheet	خيمة	khēmæ
hammer	شاكوش	shækūsh
hammock	سرير معلق	sirīr mo'allak
ice-bag	كيس ثلج	kīs tælg
kerosene	كيروسين	kirosīn
kettle	غلاية	gællææyæ
lamp	لمبة	lamba
lantern	مصباح	misbāḥ
matches	كبريت [شحيطة]	kæbrīt [shaḥḥēta]
mattress	مرتبة	mærtæbæ
methylated spirits	كحول	koḥoll
mosquito net	ناموسية	næmūsiyyæ
paraffin	كيروسين	kirosīn
penknife	مطوة	matwa

picnic case	صندوق للرحلات	sondūk lil riḥlæt
primus stove	وابور جاز	wabūr gæz
rope	حبل	ḥæbl
rucksack	شنطة للظهر	shanta lil dahr
saucepan	حلة	ḥællæ
screwdriver	مفك	mifækk
sheathknife	مطوة	matwa
sleeping bag	كيس للنوم	kis lil nōm
stove	فرن	forn
(folding) table	ترابيزة [طاولة] (للبلاج)	tarabēza [tawla] (lil plæzh)
tent	خيمة	khēmæ
tent pegs	أوتاد خيمة	æwtæd khēmæ
tent poles	عواميد خيمة	æwæmīd khēmæ
thermos flask (bottle)	ترموس	tirmos
tin opener	فتاحة علب	fættæḥit 'ilæb
tongs	زرادية	zarradiyyæ
torch	بطارية	battāriyya
water carrier	حامل للماء	ḥæmil lilmæh'
wood alcohol	كحول	koḥoll

Crockery

cups	فناجيل	fænægīl
food box	علبة طعام	ilbit taām
plates	أطباق	atbāk
saucers	أطباق للفرن	atbāk lil forn

Cutlery

forks	شوك	showæk
knives	سكاكين	sækækīn
spoons	ملاعق	mælæik
(made of) plastic	بلاستيك	plastik
(made of) stainless steel	معدنية	mæ'dæniyyæ

Chemist's (drugstore)

In the Middle East, chemists normally don't stock the great range of goods that you'll find in England or the U.S. In the window you'll see a notice telling you where the nearest all-night chemist's is.

For reading ease, this section has been divided into two parts:

1. Pharmaceutical—medicine, first-aid, etc.
2. Toiletry—toilet articles, cosmetics.

General

Where's the nearest chemist's?	أين أقرب أجزخانة [فرماشية] ؟	æynæ akrab ægzækhǣnæ [færmæshiyyæ]
What time does the chemist open/close?	متى تفتح / تقفل الاجزخانة [الفرماشية] ؟	mætǣ tæftæḥ/takfil æl 'ægzækhǣnæ [æl færmæshiyyæ]

Part 1—Pharmaceutical

I want something for...	أريد شيئاً لـ ...	orīd shæy'æn li
Can you recommend something for...?	هل يمكنك أن تنصحنى بشيء لـ ... ؟	hæl yomkinæk æn tænsaḥni bi shæy'in li
a cold/a cough	برد / سعال	bærd/soǣl
a hangover	دوخة	dōkhæ
sunburn	ضربة شمس	darbit shæms
travel sickness	دوار السفر	dowār ælsafar
Can you make up this prescription?	هل يمكنك أن تجهز لى هذه الروشيتة ؟	hæl yomkinæk æn togæhhiz li hǣzihi æl roshittæ
Shall I wait?	هل أنتظر ؟	hæl antazir
When shall I come back?	متى أرجع ؟	mætǣ argaa

FOR DOCTORS, see page 162

Can I get it without a prescription?	هل يباع بلا روشيتة ؟	hæl yobææ bilæ roshittæ
Can I have a/an/some...?	أريد ...	orīd
antiseptic cream	كريم مطهر	krēm motahhir
Band-Aids	شريط لاصق	shirīt lāsik
bandage	رباط ـ شاش	robāt-shæsh
chlorine tablets	حبوب كلور	ḥobūb klōr
corn plasters	شريط للكالو	shirīt lil kallo
cotton wool	قطن طبى	kotn tibbi
cough drops	نقط للسعلة	no'at lil sææhlæ
diabetic lozenges	سكارين	sækærīn
disinfectant	مطهر	motahhir
ear drops	نقط للاذن	no'at lil 'ozon
Elastoplast	شريط لاصق	shirīt lāsik
eye drops	قطرة للعيون	katra lil oyūn
flea powder	بودرة للبراغيث	bodra lil bæræegīt
gargle	غرغرة	gargara
gauze	شاش	shæsh
insect lotion	لوسيون ضد الحشرات	losyōn did æl ḥasharāt
insect repellent	طارد للحشرات	tārid lil ḥasharāt
iodine	يـود	yōd
laxative	ملين	molæyyin
mouthwash	غسيل للفم	gæsīl lil fæm
quinine tablets	أقراص كينين	akrās kinīn
sanitary napkins	فوط ورق طبى	fowatt warak tibbi
sleeping pills	حبوب منومة	ḥobūb monæwwimæ
stomach pills	أقراص للهضم	akrās lil hadm
thermometer	ترمومتر	tirmomitr
throat lozenges	أقراص للزور	akrās lil zōr
tissues	غيارات	giyarāt
tranquillizers	أقراص مهدئة	akrās mohæddi'æ
vitamin pills	أقراص فيتامين	akrās vitæmīn

Part 2—Toiletry

I'd like a/an/some...	أريد ...	or**ī**d
acne cream	كريم لحب الشباب	krēm li**ḥæbb** æl shæ**bææb**
after-shave lotion	لوسيون بعد الحلاقة	los**yōn** **baa**d æl ḥi**lā**ka
astringent	قابض	**kā**bid
bath salts	أملاح للحمام	æm**lææḥ** lil ḥæm**mææm**
cologne	كلونيا	ko**lo**nyææ
cream	كريم	krēm
cleansing cream	كريم للتنظيف	krēm lil tan**zīf**
cold cream	كولد كريم	kold krēm
cuticle cream	كريم لسطح الجلد	krēm li satḥ æl gild
foundation cream	كريم أساسى	krēm æ**sææ**si
moisturizing cream	كريم مرطب	krēm mo**rat**tib
night cream	كريم لليل	krēm lil lēl
deodorant	مزيل لرائحة العرق	mo**zīl** li rā'**i**ḥæt æl 'arak
emery board	مبرد أظافر كرتون	**mab**rad a**zā**fir kar**tōn**
eye pencil	قلم كحل للعين	**ka**lam koḥl lil ēn
eye shadow	ظل للعيون	zill lil o**yūn**
face flannel	فوطة لتنظيف الوجه	**fū**ta litan**zīf** æl wægh
face powder	بودرة للوجه	**bo**dra lil wægh
foot cream/powder	كريم / بودرة للقدم	krēm/**bo**dra lil **ka**dam
hand cream/lotion	كريم / لوسيون لليد	krēm/los**yōn** lil yædd
Kleenex	كلينكس	klī**niks**
lipsalve	ملون للشفايف	mo**læ**wwin lil shæ**fææ**yif
lipstick	روج للشفايف	rūzh lil shæ**fææ**yif
make-up remover pads	قصائص مزيلة للتواليت	ka**sā**'is mo**zī**læ lil twææ**litt**
mascara	كحل	koḥl
nail brush	فرشاة للاظافر	**for**shæ lil a**zā**fir
nail clippers	أصافة للاظافر	'as**sā**fa lil a**zā**fir
nail file	مبرد أظافر	**mab**rad a**zā**fir
nail polish	ملمع للاظافر	mo**læ**mmi' lil '**a**zā**fir**
nail polish remover	مزيل للون الاظافر	mo**zīl** li**lōn** æl 'a**zā**fir

nail scissors	مقص للاظافر	makass lil azāfir
oil	زيت	zēt
perfume	عطر	itr
powder	بودرة	bodra
powder puff	بخاخة بودرة	bækhkhækhit bodra
razor blades	أمواس حلاقة	æmwæs ḥilæka
rouge	أحمر شفاة	aḥmar shifæh
shampoo	شامبو	shæmpū
shaving brush	فرشاة للحلاقة	forshæ lil ḥilæka
shaving cream	كريم للحلاقة	krēm lil ḥilæka
shaving soap	صابون للحلاقة	sabūn lil ḥilæka
soap	صابون	sabūn
sponge	سفنجة	sæfingæ
sun-tan cream/oil	كريم / زيت للشمس	krēm/zēt lil shæms
talcum powder	بودرة تلك	bodra tælk
toilet paper	ورق تواليت	warak twælitt
toilet water	ماء للتواليت	mæ' lil twælitt
toothbrush	فرشاة للاسنان	forshæ lil æsnæn
toothpaste	معجون للاسنان	mæægūn lil æsnæn
towel	فوطة	fūta
wash cloth	فوطة لتنظيف الوجه	fūta litanzīf æl wægh

For your hair

brush	فرشاة	forshæ
colouring	صبغة	sabga
comb	مشط	misht
curlers	لفائف للتمويج	læfæ'if lil tæmwīg
grips	ماسكات [بنس]	mæsikæt [binæss]
lacquer	حافظ التسريحة (لاكيه)	ḥāfiz æl tæsrīḥæ (lækēh)
(bobby) pins	دبابيس للشعر	dæbæbīs lil shaar
setting lotion	سائل للتسريح	sæ'il lil tæsrīḥ

Clothing

If you want to buy something specific, prepare yourself in advance. Look at the list of clothing on page 118. Get some idea of the colour, material and size you want. They're all listed in the next few pages.

General

I'd like…	أريد …	orīd
I want … for a 10-year-old boy/girl.	أريد … لولد / لبنت عمره ١٠ سنوات .	orīd…liwælæd/libint omro 10 sænæwǣt
I want something like this.	أريد شيئاً مثل هذا .	orīd shæy'æn misl hǣzæ
I like the one in the window.	يعجبنى ما فى الفيترينة .	yo'giboni mǣ fil vitrīnæ
How much is that per metre?	بكم المتر من هذا ؟	bikæm æl mitr min hǣzæ

1 centimetre	= 0.39 in.	1 inch	= 2.54 cm.
1 metre	= 39.37 in.	1 foot	= 30.5 cm.
10 metres	= 32.81 ft.	1 yard	= 0.91 m.

Colour

I want something in…	أريد لون …	orīd lōn
I want a darker/lighter shade.	أريده أغمق / أفتح .	orīd æġmak/æftæḥ
I want something to match this.	أريد شيئاً يناسب هذا .	orīd shæy'æn yonǣsib hǣzæ
I don't like the colour.	لا يعجبنى اللون .	lǣ yo'giboni æl lōn

SHOPPING GUIDE

beige	بيج	bēzh
black	أسود	æswæd
blue	أزرق	æzrak
brown	بنى	bonni
cream	كريم	krēm
emerald	أخضر زمردى	akhdarr zomorrodī
golden	ذهبى	zæhæbī
green	أخضر	akhdarr
grey	رمادى	romādī
orange	برتقالى	bortokāli
pink	وردى	wærdī
purple	بنفسجى	bænæfsigī
red	أحمر	aḥmar
scarlet	أحمر غامق [نبيذى]	aḥmar gæemik [nibītī]
silver	فضى	faddi
white	أبيض	abyad
yellow	أصفر	asfar

مخطط
(mokhattat)

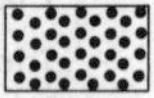
منقط
(monakkat)

مربعات
(morabbaāt)

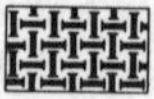
مزركش
(mozarkash)

Material

Have you anything in...?	هل عندك قماش ... ؟	hæl indæk komāsh
Is that...?	هل هذا ... ؟	hæl hææzæ
hand-embroidered	مشغول باليد	mæshgūl bil yæd
hand-made	شغل يد	shogl yæd
made here	مصنوع هنا	masnū honææ

What's it made of?

brocade	بروكار	brokār
cambric	تيل خفيف	til khæfīf
camel hair	وبر الجمل	wabar gæmæl
chiffon	شيفون	shifōn
corduroy	قطيفة مضلعة	katīfa modallaa
cotton	قطن	kotn
damask	دماسيه	dæmæsē
felt	جوخ	gūkh
flannel	فانلة	fænillæ
gabardine	جبردين	gæbærdīn
lace	دانتيل	dæntillæ
leather	جلد	gild
linen	كتان [تيل]	kittææn [til]
pique	قطن	kotn
poplin	بوبلين	poplīn
rayon	حرير صناعى	ḥærīr sinā'i
rubber	كاوتش	kæwitch
silk	حرير	ḥærīr
suede	شاموا	shæmwā
taffeta	تفتاه	tæftæ
terrycloth	قماش مسامى	omææsh mæsææmi
velvet	قطيفة	katīfa
wool	صوف	sūf

Size

I take size...	مقاسى ...	makāsī
Could you measure me?	هل يمكن أن تقيس لى ؟	hæl yomkin æn takīs li
I don't know your sizes.	لا أعرف مقاساتكم .	lææ aarif makasatkom

In that case, look at the charts on the next page.

SHOPPING GUIDE

This is your size

Ladies

Dresses/Suits						
US	10	12	14	16	18	20
Britain	32	34	36	38	40	42
Middle East	42	44	46	48	50	52

	Stockings	Shoes			
US	sizes are the same	6	7	8	9
Britain		4	5	6	7
Middle East		37	38	40	41

Gentlemen

	Suits/Overcoats						Shirts			
US / Britain	36	38	40	42	44	46	15	16	17	18
Middle East	46	48	50	52	54	56	38	41	43	45

	Shoes								
US / Britain	5	6	7	8	8	9	9	10	11
Middle East	38	39	41	42	43	43	44	44	45

Sizes may vary somewhat from country to country, so the above must be taken as an approximate guide.

A good fit?

Can I try this on?	هل يمكن أن أقيس هذا ؟	hæl **yom**kin æn a**kīs hǣ**zæ
Where's the fitting room?	أين حجرة القياس ؟	**æy**næ **ḥog**rat æl ki**yǣs**
Is there a mirror?	هل توجد مراية ؟	hæl **tū**gæd mi**rǣ**yæ

FOR NUMBERS, see page 175

It fits very well.	المقاس مضبوط جدا .	æl makās madbūt giddæn
It doesn't fit.	المقاس ليس مضبوطاً .	æl makās læysæ madbūt
It's too…	انه ... جداً ...	innæho…giddæn
short/long	قصير / طويل	kasir/tawīl
tight/loose	ضيق / واسع	dayyik/wǣsii
How long will it take to alter?	متى ينتهى التصليح ؟	mætǣ yæntæhi æl taslīḥ

Shoes

I'd like a pair of…	أريد ...	orīd
shoes/sandals/boots	حذاء / صندل / بوط	ḥizǣ'/sandal/bōt
These are too…	انه ... جداً	innæho…giddæn
narrow/wide	ضيق / واسع	dayyik/wǣsii
large/small	كبير / صغير	kæbīr/sagīr
Do you have a larger size?	هل عندك مقاس أكبر ؟	hæl indæk makās akbar
I want a smaller size.	أريد مقاس أصغر .	orīd makās asgar
Do you have the same in…?	هل عندك لون ...	hæl indæk lōn
brown/beige	بنى / بيج	bonni/bēzh
black/white	أسود / أبيض	æswæd/abyad

Shoes worn out? Here's the key to getting them fixed again…

Can you repair these shoes?	هل يمكنك اصلاح هذا الحذاء ؟	hæl yomkinæk islāḥ hǣzæ æl ḥizǣ'
Can you stitch this?	هل يمكنك تخييط هذا ؟	hæl yomkinæk takhyīt hǣzæ
I want new soles and heels.	أريد نعل و كعب جديدين .	orīd nææl wæ kææb gædidēn
When will they be ready?	متى تكون جاهزة ؟	mætǣ tækūn gæhzæ

SHOPPING GUIDE

Clothes and accessories

I'd like a/an/some...	أريد ...	orīd
bath robe	برنس	bornos
bathing cap	بونيه للبحر	bonē lil baḥr
bathing suit	بدلة بحر [مايوه]	bædlit baḥr [mæyō]
blazer	جاكته بليزر	zhækittæ blēzær
blouse	قميص حريمى	amīs ḥærīmi
boots	بوط	bōt
bow tie	كرافاته بابيون	karavatta papyōn
bra	حامل صدر [سوتيان]	ḥææmil sadr [sūtyææn]
braces (Br.)	حمالات	hæmmælææt
briefs	لباسات [شناتين]	libæsææt [shnætīn]
cap	كاسكتة	kæskittæ
cape	كابة [حرملة]	kææbæ [ḥarmala]
coat	معطف	mi'taf
costume	بدلة	bædlæ
dinner jacket	بدلة سموكنج	bædlæ smōking
dress	فستان	fostææn
dressing gown	روب	rōb
evening dress	فستان للسهرة	fostææn lil sahra
fur coat	معطف فرو	mi'taf farw
girdle	حزام	ḥizææm
gloves	جوانتى [كفوف]	gowænti [kfūf]
handkerchief	منديل	mændīl
hat	قبعة	kobbaa
jacket	جاكتة	zhækittæ
jeans	بنطلون «بلوجين»	bantalōn blū zhīnz
jersey	بلوفر	polōvar
jumper (Br.)	بلوفر	polōvar
nightdress	قميص نوم	kamīs nōm
panty-girdle	كورسيه	korsē
panty hose	شراب حريمى طويل	shorāb ḥærīmi tawīl

SHOPPING GUIDE

pyjamas	بيجامة	pizhǣmæ
raincoat	معطف مطر	mi'taf matar
sandals	صندل	sandal
scarf	اشارب	isharp
shirt	قميص	kamīs
shoes	حذاء [سباط]	ḥizǣ' [sobbāt]
shorts (Br.)	شورت	short
skirt	جوب	jūp
socks	شراب [كالسات]	shorāb [kælsǣt]
stockings	شراب حريمى	shorāb ḥærīmi
suit (man's)	بدلة	bædlæ
suit (woman's)	فستان	fostǣn
suspenders	حمالة	ḥæmmǣlæ
sweater	جاكتة	zhækittæ
tennis shoes	حذاء رياضى	ḥizǣ' riyādi
tie	كرافات	kravāt
tights	شراب حريمى طويل	shorāb ḥærīmi tawīl
trousers	بنطلون	bantalōn
underpants (men)	لباسات [شناتين]	libæsǣt [shnætīn]
undershirt	فانلة	fænillæ
vest (Am.)	صديرى	sidēri
vest (Br.)	فانلة	fænillæ
waistcoat	صديرى	sidēri

belt	حزام	ḥizǣm
buckle	توكة	tōkæ
button	زرار	zorār
collar	ياقة	yǣka
pocket	جيب	gēb
shoe laces	رباط أحذية	robāt æḥziyæ
zip (zipper)	سوستة	sostæ

Electrical appliances and accessories—Records

There is no standard voltage within any single Middle-Eastern country, let alone throughout the region as a whole. The voltages are, in general: 220 volts AC, 50 cycles in Egypt (with a few exceptions 110 volts); 220 volts AC, 50 cycles in Jordan; and 110–220 volts AC, 50 cycles in Lebanon. So check before you plug your appliance in. The plug in use throughout the Middle East is the two-round-pin type.

What's the voltage?	كم الفولت ؟	kæm æl volt
I want a plug for this.	أريد بريزة لهذا .	orīd prīzæ lihǣzæ
Do you have a battery for this.	هل عندك بطارية لهذا ؟	hæl indæk battāriyyæ lihǣzæ
This is broken. Can you repair it?	هذا مكسور . هل يمكنك اصلاحه ؟	hǣzæ mæksūr. hæl yomkinæk islāḥoh
When will it be ready?	متى يكون جاهزاً ؟	mǣtæ yækūn gǣhizæn
I'd like a/an/some...	أريد ...	orīd
adapter	بريزة أمريكانى	prīzæ æmrikǣni
battery	بطارية	battāriyyæ
blender	خلاط	khallāt
food mixer	خلاط	khallāt
hair dryer	منشف الشعر [سشوار]	monæshshif shaar [sishwār]
iron	مكواة	mækwæ
kettle	غلاية	gællǣyæ
plug	بريزة	prīzæ
radio	راديو	radyo
portable	ترانزيستور	tranzistor
record player	بيك آب	pik-ap
portable	ترانزيستور	tranzistor
shaver	ماكينة حلاقة	mækinit ḥilāka
speakers	مكبرات صوت	mokæbbirǣt sōt

SHOPPING GUIDE

tape recorder	ريكوردر	rikordær
cassette	كاسيت	kasitt
toaster	توستر	tostær
transformer	محول [ترانس]	moḥæwwil [trans]

Record shop

Do you have any records by…	هل عندك اسطوانات لـ..؟	hæl indæk istiwanāt li
Can I listen to this record?	أريد أن أسمع هذه الاسطوانة من فضلك.	orīd æn æsmæ' hæzihi æl istiwāna min fadlak
I'd like a cassette.	أريد كاسيت.	orīd kasitt
I want a new stylus.	أريد ابرة جديدة.	orīd ibra gædīdæ

33 rpm	٣٣ لفة	tælātæ wæ tælætīn læffæ
45 rpm	٤٥ لفة	khæmsæ wæ ærbi'īn læffæ
mono/stereo	مونو / ستريو	mōno/stiryō

Arabic music	موسيقى عربية	mūsīka arabiyyæ
classical music	موسيقى كلاسيك	mūsīka klæsīk
folk music	موسيقى فولكلورية	mūsīka folklōriyyæ
instrumental music	موسيقى	mūsīka
jazz	موسيقى جاز	mūsīka zhæz
light music	موسيقى خفيفة	mūsīka khæfīfæ
orchestral music	موسيقى جماعية	mūsīka gæmæ'iyyæ
pop music	موسيقى غربية	mūsīka garbiyya

Hairdressing – At the barber's

I'm in a hurry.	أنا مستعجل .	ænǣ **mista'**gil
I want a haircut, please.	أريد قص الشعر من فضلك .	or**ī**d 'ass il **shaar** min **fad**lak
I'd like a shave.	أريد حلق الذقن .	or**ī**d ḥælk æl zækn
Don't cut it too short.	لا تقصه قصيراً جداً .	lǣ ta'**osso** kas**ī**ran **gid**dæn
Scissors only, please.	المقص فقط من فضلك .	æl mæ'**ass fa**katt min **fad**lak
A razor cut, please.	قص بالموس من فضلك .	'oss bil mūs min **fad**lak
Don't use the clippers.	لا تستعمل الماكينة .	læ tæst**æ**æmil æl **mæ**kinæ
Just a trim, please.	قص بسيط من فضلك .	'ass ba**sīt** min **fad**lak
That's enough off.	يكفى هذا القص .	**yæ**kfi **hǣ**zæ æl 'ass
A little more off the…	قصر أكثر من …	**kas**sar **ak**tar min
back	الخلف	æl khælf
neck	الخلف	æl khælf
sides	الجوانب	æl gæ**wǣ**nib
top	أعلى	**æ**ælǣ
I don't want any oil.	لا أريد زيت [بريانتين] .	lǣ or**ī**d zēt [briyantīn]
Would you please trim my…?	أريد توضيب الـ … من فضلك .	orīd tawdīb æl… min **fad**lak
beard	ذقن	zækn
moustache	شنب	**shæ**næbb
sideboards (sideburns)	سوالف	sæ**wǣ**lif
Thank you. That's fine.	شكرا . هذا حسن .	shokran. **hǣ**zæ **ḥæ**sin
How much do I owe you?	كم الحساب ؟	kæm æl ḥi**sǣb**
This is for you.	هذا لك .	**hǣ**zæ læk

FOR TIPPING, see inside back cover

SHOPPING GUIDE

Ladies' hairdressing

Is there a hairdresser's in the hotel?	هل يوجد صالون تجميل فى الفندق ؟	hæl yūgæd salōn tægmīl fil fondok
Can I make an appointment for sometime on Thursday?	أريد موعداً ليوم الخميس من فضلك .	orīd mæw'id liyōm æl khæmīs min fadlak
I'd like it cut and shaped.	أريد قص وتسريح .	orīd 'ass wæ tæsrīḥ
with a fringe (bangs)	بفرانجة من الامام	bi franzha minæl 'æmææm
a razor cut	قص بالموس	'ass bil mūs
a re-style	تسريحة جديدة	tæsrīḥæ gædīdæ
with ringlets	ببوكلات	bi boklææt
with waves	مموج	momæwwæg
in a bun	شينيون	shinyōn
I want (a)...	أريد ...	orīd
bleach	ازالة اللون	izææIit æl lōn
colour rinse	غسيل باللون	gæsīl bil lōn
dye	صباغة [تلوين]	sibāga [tælwīn]
permanent	برماننت	pirmanant
shampoo and set	شامبو وتسريح	shampū wæ tæsrīḥ
tint	لون	lōn
touch up	لمسات	læmæsææt
the same colour	نفس اللون	næfs æl lōn
a darker colour	لون أغمق	lōn ægmak
a lighter colour	لون أفتح	lōn æftæḥ
auburn/blond/brunette	بنى / أشقر / أسود	bonnī/ash'ar/æswæd
Do you have a colour chart?	هل عندك دليل للالوان ؟	hæl indæk dælīl lil ælwææn
I want a...	أريد ...	orīd
manicure/pedicure	مانيكير / بديكير	mænikūr/pidikūr
face-pack	شد للوجه	shædd lil wægh

FOR DAYS OF THE WEEK, see page 181

Jeweller's—Watchmaker's

Since the days of the pharaohs, handcrafting jewellery has been considered an honoured profession. Moreover, a woman's social status was reflected in the number of jewels she wore. In the markets and jewellery shops of the Middle East, you'll find excellent copies of ancient jewellery—slave bracelets, bangles, snake-shaped bracelets, bedouins' necklaces. Due to cheap local labour, you'll be pleasantly surprised at how inexpensive much jewellery can be. Don't forget, this is the occasion to try your skill at haggling.

Can you repair this watch?	هل يمكنك اصلاح هذه الساعة ؟	hæl yomkinæk islāḥ hǣzihi æl sǣæ
The ... is broken.	الـ ... مكسور .	æl...maksūr
glass/spring	زجاج / زمبلك [سوستة]	zogǣg/zæmbælik [sostæ]
strap/winder	أستيك / مسمار	ostēk/mosmār
I want this watch cleaned.	أريد تنظيف هذه الساعة .	orīd tanzīf hǣzihi æl sǣæ
When will it be ready?	متى تكون جاهزة ؟	mætæ tækūn gæhzæ
Could I please see that?	من فضلك اكشف على هذا .	min fadlak ikshif ælæ hǣzæ
I want a small present for...	أريد هدية صغيرة لـ ...	orīd hædiyyæ sagīra li
I don't want anything too expensive.	لا أريد شيئاً غالياً .	læ orīd shæy'æn gǣliyæn
I want something...	أريد شيئاً . . .	orīd shæy'æn
better/cheaper/simpler	أحسن / أرخص / أبسط	æḥsæn/arkhas/absat
Is this real silver?	هل هذا فضة حقيقية ؟	hæl hǣzæ fidda ḥakikiyya
Have you anything in gold?	هل عندك شيئاً من ذهب ؟	hæl indæk shæy'an min zæhæb
How many carats is this?	كم قيراط ؟	kæm kirāt

When you go to a jeweller's, you've probably got some idea of what you want beforehand. Find out what the article is made of and then look up the name for the article itself in the following lists.

What's it made of?

alabaster	الباستر	alabastar
amethyst	رجمشت	rægmæsht
brass	نحاس أصفر	niḥǣs asfar
copper	نحاس	niḥǣs
coral	مرجان	morgǣn
crystal	كريستال	kristǣl
cut glass	زجاج مشكل	zogǣg moshækkæl
diamond	الماس	almās
ebony	أبنوس	æbænōs
emerald	زمرد	zomorrod
enamel	صدف	sadaf
glass	زجاج	zogǣg
gold	ذهب	zæhæb
gold plate	مذهب	mozæhhæb
ivory	عاج	ǣg
jade	جاد	zhǣd
mother-of-pearl	صدف	sadaf
onyx	عقيق	akīk
pearl	لولى	lūli
pewter	معدن	mæædæn
platinum	بلاتين	plǣtīn
ruby	ياقوت	yǣ'ūt
sapphire	ياقوت أزرق	yǣ'ūt æzrak
silver	فضة	fidda
silver plate	مفضض	mofaddad
topaz	زبرجد	zæbærgæd
turquoise	فيروز	færūz

What is it?

beads	خرز	kharazz
bracelet	غويشة	giwēshæ
brooch	بروش	brōsh
chain	سلسلة	silsilæ
charm	حلية	ḥilyæ
cigarette case	علبة سجاير	ilbit sægǣyir
cigarette lighter	ولاعة [قداحة]	wællǣæ [æddǣḥæ]
clock	ساعة حائط	sǣ'it ḥā'it
alarm clock	منبه	minæbbih
cross	صليب	salīb
cuff-links	زراير قمصان	zarāyir komsān
cutlery	فضية للاكل	faddiyya lil 'ækl
earrings	حلق	ḥælæk
jewel box	علبة جواهر	ilbit gæwǣhir
necklace	عقد	okd
pendant	علّيقة	ollē'æ
pin	دبوس	dæbbūs
powder compact	علبة بودرة	ilbit bodra
ring	خاتم	khǣtim
engagement ring	دبلة خطوبة	diblit khotūba
puzzle ring	خاتم من قطع كثيرة	khǣtim min kitaa kæsīra
signet ring	خاتم رجالى	khǣtim rigæli
wedding ring	دبلة	diblæ
rosary	سبحة [مسبحة]	sibḥæ [mæsbæḥæ]
silverware	فضية	faddiyya
strap	غويشة	gowēshæ
watch strap	أستيك ساعة	ostēk sǣæ
tie-clip	دبوس كرافات	dæbbūs kravāt
watch	ساعة	sǣæ
pocket watch	ساعة جيب	sǣ'it gēb
wrist-watch	ساعة يد	sǣ'it yædd

Laundry—Dry cleaning

If your hotel doesn't have its own laundry/dry cleaning service, ask the porter:

Where's the nearest laundry/dry cleaner's?	أين أقرب محل غسيل ومكوة / تنظيف ؟	æynæ **akrab** mæ**ḥæll** gæ**sīl** wæ **mæk**wæ / tan**zīf**
I want these clothes...	أريد ... هذه الملابس .	o**rīd**... **hæ**zihi æl mæ**læ**bis
cleaned	تنظيف	tan**zīf**
pressed/ironed	مكوة	**mæk**wit
washed	غسيل	gæ**sīl**
When will it be ready?	متى تكون جاهزة ؟	**mæ**tæ tæ**kūn gæ**hizæ
I need it...	أريدها ...	orī**do**hæ
today	اليوم	æl yōm
tomorrow	بكرة	**bok**ra
before Thursday	قبل يوم الخميس	kabl yōm æl khæ**mīs**
Can you ... this?	أريد ... هذا من فضلك .	o**rīd**... **hæ**zæ min **fad**lak
mend/patch/stitch	رفة / ترقيع / خياطة	**ræf**fit/tær**kī'**/khi**yā**tit
Can you sew on this button?	هل يمكنك أن تخيط لى هذا الزر [زرار] ؟	hæl yom**ki**næk æn to**khay**yit lī **hæ**zæ æl zirr [zo**rār**]
Can you get this stain out?	هل يمكنك ازالة هذه البقعة ؟	hæl yom**ki**næk i**zæ**lit **hæ**zihi æl **bo**kaa
Can this be invisibly mended?	هل يمكنك رفة هذا دون أن يظهر ؟	hæl yom**ki**næk **ræf**fit **hæ**zæ **dū**næ æn **yaz**har
This isn't mine.	هذا ليس ملكى .	**hæ**zæ **læy**sæ **mil**kī
There's one piece missing.	ناقص قطعة .	**nā**kis **kit**'a
There's a hole in this.	يوجد ثقب [خرم] فى هذا .	**yū**gæd sokb [khorm] fī **hæ**zæ
Is my laundry ready?	هل غسيلى جاهز ؟	hæl gæ**sī**li **gæ**hiz

Photography—Cameras

The basic still and home movie exposures are usually given in English in the instructions with the roll.

I want an inexpensive camera.	أريد كاميرا رخيصة .	orīd kæmira rakhīsa

Film

I'd like a...	أريد ...	orīd
cartridge	كارتردج [خزنة الفيلم]	kartridzh [khæznit ilfilm]
film for this camera	فيلم لهذه الكاميرا	film lihæzihi æl kæmira
a ... film	فيلم ...	film
120	١٢٠	miyyæ wæ 'ishrīn
127	١٢٧	miyyæ sæb'æ wæ 'ishrīn
135	١٣٥	miyyæ khæmsæ wæ tælætīn
620	٦٢٠	sottomiyyæ wæ 'ishrīn
8-mm	٨ مم	tæmænyæ milli
super 8	سوبر ٨ مم	sūpar tæmænyæ milli
16-mm	١٦ مم	sittāshar milli
20 exposures	٢٠ صورة	'ishrīn sūra
36 exposures	٣٦ صورة	sittæ wæ tælætīn sūra
this ASA/DIN number	درجة الحساسية ازا / دين	daragit il ḥæsæsiyyæ aza/din
fast/fine grain	سريع / قليل الحساسية	særīi/kalīl æl hæsæsiyyæ
black and white	أسود وأبيض	'iswid wabyad
colour	ألوان	'ælwæn
colour negative	نجاتيف بالالوان	nigætīf bil 'ælwæn
colour slide	سلايد بالالوان	slayd bil 'ælwæn
artificial light type	للضوء الصناعى	lil dō' æl sinā'i
daylight type	لضوء النهار	lidō' æl nahār

FOR NUMBERS, see page 175

Processing

How much do you charge for developing?	بكم التحميض ؟	bikæm æl taḥmīd
I want ... prints of each negative.	أريد ... صورة من كل سلبية [نجاتيف] .	orīd...sūra min kol sælbiyyæ [nigætif]

Accessories

I want a/an/some...	أريد ...	orīd
cable release	مفتاح التصوير الآلي	moftāḥ æl taswīr æl'ǣli
exposure meter	مقياس فتحة العدسة	mikyǣs fæthit æl'ædæsæ
flash bulbs	لمبات الفلاش	lambāt æl flǣsh
flash cubes	لمبات فلاش مكعبة	lambāt flǣsh mokæ'æbæ
filter	فلتر	filtar
red/yellow	أحمر / أصفر	'aḥmar/'asfar
ultra violet	فوق البنفسجي	fō' æl bænæfsigi
lens cap	غطاء العدسة	gitā' æl 'ædæsæ
lens cleaners	منظف العدسة	monazzif lil 'ædæsæ

Broken

Can you repair this camera?	هل يمكنك اصلاح هذه الكاميرا ؟	hæl yomkinæk 'islāḥ hēzihi æl kæmira
The film is jammed.	الفيلم محشور .	æl film maḥshūr
There's something wrong with the...	الـ ... عطلان .	æl...'atlān
exposure counter	عداد الصور	'æddǣd æl sowar
film winder	مفتاح لف الفيلم	moftāḥ læff æl film
lens	عدسة	'ædæsæ
light meter	مقياس الضوء	mikyǣs æl dō'
rangefinder	ضابط المسافة	dābit æl mæsǣfæ
shutter	منظم فتحة العدسة	monazzim fæthit æl 'ædæsæ

Provisions

I'd like a/an/some... please.	أريد ... من فضلك .	orīd...min fadlak
apples	تفاح	toffæḥ
bananas	موز	mōz
beer	بيرة	bīræ
biscuits (Br.)	بسكويت	bæskæwīt
bread	عيش [خبز]	ēsh [khobz]
butter	زبدة	zibdæ
cake	كيك	kēk
candy	حلويات	ḥælæwiyyæt
cheese	جبنة	gibnæ
chocolate	شيكولاته	shokolāta
coffee	قهوة [بن]	kahwa [bonn]
cold cuts	لحوم باردة	loḥūm bærdæ
cookies	بسكويت	bæskæwīt
cooking fat	سمن	sæmnæ
cream	كريمة	krēmæ
eggs	بيض	bēd
ice-cream	آيس كريم [جيلاتي]	æys krēm [zhilāti]
lemonade	لمونادة	læmonǣtæ
lemons	ليمون [حامض]	læmūn [ḥāmid]
lettuce	خس	khass
milk	لبن حليب	læbæn ḥælīb
mustard	مستردة	mostarda
oranges	برتقال	bortokāl
pepper	فلفل [بهار]	filfil [bohār]
potatoes	بطاطس	batātis
rolls	خبز سندوتش	khobz sændæwitsh
salad	صلاطة	salāta
salt	ملح	mælḥ
sandwiches	سندوتش	sændæwitsh
sausages	سوسيس [سجق/معانق]	sōsīs [sogo'/mæ'ǣnik]

sugar	سكر	**sok**kar
sweets	حلويات	hælæwiy**yǣt**
tea	شاى	shǣy
tomatoes	طماطم [بندورة]	ta**mā**tim [bana**dū**ra]
yogurt	زبادى [لبن]	zæ**bǣ**di [**læ**bæn]

And don't forget...

a bottle opener	فتاحة زجاجات	fæt**tǣ**ḥit zo**gǣgǣt**
a corkscrew	فتاحة علب	fæt**tǣ**ḥit ilæb
matches	كبريت [شحيطة]	kæb**rīt** [shaḥ**ḥā**tæ]
paper napkins	فوط ورق	**fo**watt **wæ**ræk
a tin (can) opener	فتاحة علب	fæt**tǣ**hit ilæb

Weights and measures

1 kilogram or kilo (kg) = 1000 grams (g)

100 g = 3.5 oz. ½ kg = 1.1 lb. 1 oz. = 28.35 g
200 g = 7.0 oz. 1 kg = 2.2 lb. 1 lb. = 453.60 g

1 litre (l) = 0.88 imp. quarts = 1.06 U.S. quarts
1 imp. quart = 1.14 l 1 U.S. quart = 0.95 l
1 imp. gallon = 4.55 l 1 U.S. gallon = 3.8 l

box	علبة	ilbæ
carton	صندوق كارتون	son**dūk** kar**tōn**
jar	أبريق	æb**rī'**
packet	باكو	**bǣ**ko
tin (can)	علبة صفيح	ilbæ sa**fiḥ**
tube	أنبوبة	onbūbæ
gram	جرام	grām
pound	رطل	ratl
kilogram	كيلوجرام	kilo**grām**
litre	لتر	litr

Souvenirs

Browsing through the bustling markets will turn up countless treasured souvenirs of your visit to the Middle East. Jewellery and precious stones will certainly interest the ladies. Ceramics, glassware, sandals and hand-embroidered garments also make especially appreciated gifts.

Below are a few suggestions for souvenirs you might like to bring home:

antiques	انتيكات	æntik**ææt**
backgammon set	طاولة زهر	**tawlit** zahr
brass and copper objects	مصنوعات نحاس	masnū'**ät** ni**ḥææs**
carpets	سجاجيد	sæg**ææ**gīd
ceramics	فخار	fokh**khār**
cutlery (Lebanon)	فضية	fad**diyya**
dagger	خنجر	**khan**gar
glass (hand-blown)	زجاج	zo**gææg**
gold filigree	ذهب مشغول	dæhæb mæsh**gūl**
hand-embroidered garments	ملابس تطريز يدوى	mæl**ææ**bis tatrīz yædæwi
handicrafts	صناعات يدوية	sina**āt** gildiyyæ
jewellery	مجوهرات	mogawhar**āt**
kaftan	قفطان	kof**tān**
leather goods	مصنوعات جلدية	masnū'**āt** gildiyyæ
nargile (water pipe)	شيشة [أرجيلة]	**shī**shæ [ær**gī**læ]
oriental lamp	مصباح شرقى	mis**bāḥ** **shar**ki
sandals	صندل	**san**dal
silver jewel box	علبة جواهر فضة	ilbit gæw**ææ**hir **fad**da
stones, precious	أحجار كريمة	aḥ**gār** kæ**rī**mæ
semi-precious	شبه كريمة	shibh kæ**rī**mæ
tarboosh (fez)	طربوش	tar**būsh**
Turkish coffee service	طقم للقهوة التركى	takm lil **kah**wa æl **tor**ki

Tobacconist's

You'll find the typical oriental cigarettes (e.g., *Cleopatra* in Egypt, *Bafra* or *Khanon* in Lebanon) lighter than those at home. The reason is that the young tobacco leaves are harvested before they mature. Brands that are manufactured locally are quite cheap. Foreign cigarettes are considerably more expensive.

Give me a/an some..., please.	أريد ... من فضلك .	orīd... min **fad**lak
cigars	سيجار	sigār
cigarette case	عابة لحمل السجاير	'ilbæ liḥæml æl sægǣyir
cigarette holder	فم سجاير	fomm sægǣyir
flints	حجر ولاعة [قداحة]	ḥagar wællǣæ ['æddǣḥæ]
lighter	ولاعة [قداحة]	wællǣæ ['æddǣḥæ]
lighter fluid/gas	بنزين / غاز ولاعة [قداحة]	bænzīn/gǣz wællǣæ ['æddǣḥæ]
matches	كبريت [شحيطة]	kæbrīt [shaḥḥēta]
packet of cigarettes	علبة سجاير	'ilbit sægǣyir
packet of *Cleopatras*	علبة كليوباترة	'ilbit kilyōbatra
pipe	بايب	payp
pipe tobacco	دخان بايب	dokh**kaǣn** payp
pipe cleaners	منظف بايب	monazzif payp
tobacco pouch	باكو دخان بايب	**bǣ**ko dokh**khǣn** payp
Have you any...?	عندك ... ؟	ændæk
American cigarettes	سجاير أمريكانى	sægǣyir 'æmrikǣni
English cigarettes	سجاير انجليزى	sægǣyir 'ingilīzi
menthol cigarettes	سجاير منتول	sægǣyir mintol
I'd like a carton.	أريد خرطوشة .	orīd khartūsha

filter-tipped	بفم فلتر	bifomm filtær
without filter	بدون فلتر	bidūn filtær

Your money: banks—currency

In the Middle East, there's generally no import limit on foreign currency. In Egypt, all foreign currency brought in must be declared. When you change money, don't forget to ask for a receipt or have the transaction noted on your D (declaration) form. When leaving Egypt, customs will ask you either for your receipts or your D form.

Monetary unit

Egypt: 1 Egyptian pound (£E) = 100 piastres (pts.) = 1,000 *milliemes* (mmes.)

Banknotes: 5, 10, 25 and 50 pts.; £E 1, 5, 10, 20 and 100
Coins: 5 and 10 pts.

Jordan: 1 Jordanian dinar (JD) = 1,000 fils (fls.)

Banknotes: 500 fls.; JD 1, 5, 10, 20
Coins: 1, 5, 10, 20, 25, 50, 100, 250 and 500 fls.

Lebanon: 1 Lebanese pound (£L) = 100 piastres (pts.)
Banknotes: £L 1, 5, 10, 25, 50, 100 and 250
Coins: 5, 10, 25 and 50 pts.

Banking hours

Egypt: 8.30 a.m. – 12.30 p.m., daily except Friday; Sunday 10 a.m. to noon.

Jordan: 8 a.m. – 2 p.m.; Saturday to Thursday.

Lebanon: 8.30 a.m. – 12.30 p.m., Monday to Friday; Saturday 8.30 a.m. – 12 a.m.

Before going

Where's the nearest...? bank/currency exchange?	أين أقرب بنك / مكتب كامبيو ؟	æynæ 'akrab bænk/ mæktæb kæmbyo
Where can I cash a traveller's cheque (check)?	أين يمكن صرف شيكات سياحية ؟	æynæ yomkin sarf shēkæt siyæḥiyyæ
Where's the American Express?	أين الأميريكان اكسبريس؟	æynæ æl 'æmirikæn iksprēs

Inside

I want to change some dollars/pounds.	أريد تحويل دولارات / جنيهات استرليني .	orīd tæḥwīl dolārāt/ gonæyhæt 'istirlīni
What's the exchange rate?	ما سعر التحويل ؟	mæ siir æl tæḥwīl
What rate of commission do you charge?	ما العمولة التى يأخذها البنك ؟	mæ æl 'omulæ ællæti yæ'khozohæ æl bænk
Can you cash a personal cheque?	هل تصرف شيكات خاصة ؟	hæl tasrif shēkæt khāssa
How long will it take to clear?	ما طول مدة المراجعة ؟	mæ tūl moddit æl moræg'æ
Can you wire my bank in London?	هل يمكنك أن ترسل تلغراف الى بنكى فى لندن ؟	hæl yomkinæk æn torsil tælligrāf 'ilæ bænki fi landan
I have...	عندى ...	'indi
a letter of credit	خطاب ضمان	khitāb damān
an introduction from...	خطاب من ...	khitāb min
a credit card	بطاقة رصيد مصرفى	bitākit rasid masrafi
I'm expecting some money from... Has it arrived yet?	أنا منتظر فلوس من ... هل وصلت ؟	ænæ montazir folūs min... hæl wasalæt
Please give me... 10-pound notes (bills) and some small change.	من فضلك اعطنى ... ورقة من فئة العشرة جنيهات وبعض الفكـّة [الفراطة]	min fadlak aatini... waraka min fi'æt 10 gonæyhæt wa baad æl fækkæ [æl frāta]

Give me... large notes and the rest in small notes.	اعطنى ... ورقة من فئة كبيرة والباقى فئات صغيرة.	aatinī... waraka min fi'æ kæbīræ wæl bāki fi'ǣt sagīra
Could you please check that again?	من فضلك راجع هذا .	min fadlak rǣgii hǣzæ
I want to credit this to my account.	أريد ايداع هذا فى حسابى .	orīd 'idǣæ hǣzæ fi ḥisǣbi
Where should I sign?	أين أوقع ؟	æynæ owakki'

Currency converter

In a world of fluctuating currencies, we can offer no more than this do-it-yourself chart. You can get a card showing current exchange rates from banks, travel agents and tourist offices. Why not fill in this chart, too, for handy reference?

	£	$
10 Egyptian piastres		
50		
1 Egyptian pound		
5		
10		
100 Jordanian fils		
500		
1 Jordanian dinar		
5		
10		
1 Lebanese pound		
5		
10		
50		
100		

At the post office

In Egypt post offices are open from 8.30 a.m. to 3 p.m. except Friday. Big hotels usually have all post office facilities at the reception.

In Jordan the post offices are open from 8 a.m. to 2 p.m. except Friday when they are closed all day.

In Lebanon, mail, telex and telegram service is available from 8.30 a.m. to 1 p.m. except Friday.

Where's the nearest post office?	أين أقرب مكتب بريد ؟	æynæ **akrab mæktæb** bæ**rīd**
What time does the post office open/ close?	متى يفتح / يقفل مكتب البريد ؟	mætæ **yæftæḥ/yakfil** mæktæb æl bærīd
What window do I go to for stamps?	أين شباك الطوابع ؟	æynæ shib**bæk** æl tawābii
At which counter can I cash an international money order?	فى أى شباك يمكننى صرف حوالة بريدية أجنبية ؟	min æyy shib**bæk** yom**ki**noni sarf ho**wæ**læ bæ**ri**diyyæ ægnæ**biy**yæ
I want some stamps, please.	أريد طوابع من فضلك .	o**rid** ta**wā**bi' min **fad**lak
What's the postage for a letter to England?	بكم الخطاب لانجلترا ؟	bi**kæm** ælkhi**tāb** li 'ingil**tira**
What's the postage for a postcard to the U.S.A.?	ما الثمن لارسال كارت بوستال الى أمريكا ؟	**mæ** æltæmæn li 'ir**sæl** kært pos**tæl** 'ilæ 'æmrikæ

طوابع	STAMPS
طرود	PARCELS
حوالات بريدية	MONEY ORDERS

Do all letters go airmail?	هل كـل الخطابات تسافر بالبريد الجوى ؟	hæl koll æl khitābāt tosǣfir bil bærīd æl gæwwi
I want to send this parcel.	أريد ارسال هذا الطرد .	orīd 'irsǣl hǣzæl tard
Do I need to fill in a customs declaration?	هل يجب أن أملأ استمارة الجمرك ؟	hæl yægib æn 'æmlæ' 'istimārit æl gomrok
Where's the mail-box?	أين صندوق الخطابات ؟	æynæ sondūk æl khitābāt
I want to send this by...	أريد ارسال هذا ...	orīd 'irsǣl hǣzæ
airmail	بالبريد الجوى	bil bærīd æl gæwwi
express (special delivery)	بالبريد المستعجل	bil bærīd æl mostæææ̈gæl
registered mail	بالبريد المسجل	bil bærīd æl mosæggæl
Where's the poste restante (general delivery)?	أين مكتب تسليم الخطابات ؟	æynæ mæktæb tæslīm æl khitābāt
Is there any mail for me? My name is...	هل توجد خطابات لى ؟ اسمى ...	hæl tūgæd kitābāt li? 'ismi
Here's my passport.	هذا باسبورى .	hǣzæ paspōri

Telegrams

I want to send a telegram. May I please have a form?	أريد ارسال تلغراف . من فضلك اعطنى استمارة .	orīd 'irsǣl tælligrāf. min fadlak aatini 'istimāra
How much is it per word?	بكم الكلمة ؟	bikæm æl kilmæ
How long will a cable to Boston take?	متى يصل التلغراف الى بوسطون ؟	mætǣ yasil æl tælligrāf 'ilǣ boston
I'd like to reverse the charges.	أريد أن يدفع المستلم ثمن التلغراف .	orīd 'æn yædfææ æl mostælim tæmæn æl tælligrāf
I'd like to send a letter-telegram (night-letter).	أريد ارسال تلغراف L.T. .	orīd 'irsǣl tælligrāf æl ti

Telephoning

You won't find any telephone booths in Egypt and Jordan except at the post office. When you want to make a local call, you can go into a store. If you want to call long distance, you'll have to go to a post office or a big hotel.

In Lebanon calls can be made from telephone booths or from restaurants, cafés or hotels. Public telephones are coin operated: insert the appropriate coins and then dial. When the other person answers, push the white button to complete the connection.

Where's the telephone?	أين التليفون ؟	æynæl tilifōn
May I use your phone?	هل يمكننى استعمال التليفون ؟	hæl yomkinoni 'istiimæl æl tilifōn
Do you have a telephone directory of Beirut?	هل عندك دليل تليفونات بيروت ؟	hæl 'indæk dælīl tilifōnæt bæyrūt
Can you help me get this number?	من فضلك ساعدنى فى الاتصال بهذا الرقم .	min fadlak sæ'idni fil 'ittisāl bihæzæ æl rakam

Operator

Do you speak English?	هل تتكلم انجليزى ؟	hæl tætækællæm ingilīzi
Good morning, I want Cairo 123456.	صباح الخير . أريد القاهرة ١٢٣٤٥٦ .	sabāḥ æl khēr. orīd ælkāhira 123 456
Can I dial direct?	هل يوجد خط مباشر ؟	hæl yūgæd khatt mobæshir
I want to place a personal (person-to-person) call.	أريد مكالمة شخصية .	orīd mokælmæ shakhsiyyæ
I want to reverse the charges.	أريد أن يدفع الشخص المطلوب ثمن المكالمة .	orīd æn yædfææ æl shakhs æl matlūb tæmæn æl mokælmæ
Will you tell me the cost of the call afterwards?	هل يمكنك أن تخبرنى بثمن المكالمة فيما بعد ؟	hæl yomkinæk æn tokhbirni bitæmæn æl mokælmæ fimæ bææd

Speaking

Hello. This is... speaking.	آلو . أنا ..	ælō. 'ænæ
I want to speak to...	أريد أن أتحدث الى ...	orīd æn 'ætæḥæddæs 'ilæ
Would you put me through to...?	من فضلك اعطنى ... ؟	min fadlak aatini
I want extension...	أريد الداخلى رقم ...	orīd æl dākhili rakam
Is that...?	هل هذا ... ؟	hæl hææzæ

Bad luck

Would you please try again later?	من فضلك حاول مرة أخرى فيما بعد .	min fadlak ḥææwil marra 'okhra fīmæ bææd
Operator, you gave me the wrong number.	لقد أعطيتنى نمرة غلط .	lakad aataytæni nimræ galat
Operator, we were cut off.	انقطعت المكالمة .	'inkata'æt æl mokælmæ

Not there

When will he/she be back?	متى يرجع / ترجع ؟	mætæ yærgaa/tærgaa
Will you tell him/her I called?	من فضلك قل له / لها انى اتصلت .	min fadlak kol læho/læhæ inni ittasalt
My name's...	اسمى ...	ismi
Would you ask him/her to call me?	من فضلك اطلب منه / منها الاتصال بى .	min fadlak otlob minho/minhæ æl 'ittisāl bī
Would you please take a message?	من فضلك خذ هذه الرسالة .	min fadlak khozz hæzihi æl risææl æ

Charges

What was the cost of that call?	بكم هذه المكالمة ؟	**bikæm** hæzihi æl mok**æ**lmæ
I want to pay for the call.	أريد أن أدفع ثمن المكالمة .	or**id** 'æn 'æ**d**fææ t**æ**mæn æl mok**æ**lmæ

توجد مكالمة تليفونية لك .	There's a telephone call for you.
ما النمرة التى تطلبها ؟	What number are you calling?
الخط مشغول .	The line's engaged.
لا يرد أحد .	There's no answer.
النمرة غلط .	You've got the wrong number.
التليفون عطلان .	The phone is out of order.
هو خرج / هى خرجت .	He's/She's out at the moment.

FOR SPELLING, see page 11

The car

Filling station

We'll start this section by considering your possible needs at a filling station.

Where's the nearest filling station?	أين أقرب محطة بنزين ؟	æynæ **akrab** ma**ḥattit** bæn**zīn**
I want...litres of petrol (gas), please.	أريد ... لتر بنزين من فضلك .	o**rīd**...litr bæn**zīn** min **fad**lak
ten/twenty/fifty	عشرة / عشرين / خمسين	**'ashara/'ishrīn/khæmsīn**
I want...litres of standard/premium.	أريد ... لتر بنزين عادى / سوبر .	o**rīd**...litr bæn**zīn** **'ǣdi**/ **sū**par
Fill the tank, please.	املأها من فضلك .	im**lǣ**hæ min **fad**lak
Please check the oil and water.	من فضلك اكشف على الزيت والماء .	min **fad**lak **ik**shif æ**lǣ** æl **zēt** wæl **mǣ'**
Give me...litres of oil.	اعطنى ... لتر زيت .	**'ātīni**...litr **zēt**
Fill up the battery with distilled water.	املأ البطارية بماء مقطّر .	**im**læ' æl bat**tā**riyya bi**may**ya mo**kat**tara
Check the brake fluid.	اكشف على زيت الفرامل .	**ik**shif æ**lǣ** **zēt** æl fa**rā**mil

Fluid measures					
litres	imp. gal.	U.S. gal.	litres	imp. gal.	U.S. gal.
5	1.1	1.3	30	6.6	7.9
10	2.2	2.6	35	7.7	9.2
15	3.3	4.0	40	8.8	10.6
20	4.4	5.3	45	9.9	11.9
25	5.5	6.6	50	11.0	13.2

CAR—SERVICE STATION

FOR NUMBERS, see page 175

Would you check the tires?	من فضلك اكشف على ضغط العجل [الدواليب] .	min **fad**lak **'ikshif** 'ælǣ dagt æl 'ægæl [æl dwælīb]
The pressure should be 23 front, 26 rear.	الضغط ٢٣ للأمام و ٢٦ للخلف .	æl dagt 23 lil 'æ**mǣm** wæ 26 lil khælf
Check the spare tire, too, please.	من فضلك اكشف على الاستبن .	min **fad**lak **'ikshif** 'ælæl 'istibn
Can you mend this puncture (fix this flat)?	من فضلك اصلح هذه العجلة [الدولاب] .	min **fad**lak **'asliḥ hǣzihi** æl 'ægælæ [æl dū**lǣb**]
Will you change this tire, please?	من فضلك غيّر هذه العجلة [الدولاب] .	min **fad**lak **gæyyir hǣzihi** æl 'ægælæ [æl dū**lǣb**]
Will you clean the windshield (windscreen)?	من فضلك نظف الزجاج الأمامى .	min **fad**lak **nazzif** æl **zogǣg** æl 'æ**mǣ**mi
Have you a road map of this area?	هل عندك خريطة للطرق فى هذه المنطقة .	hæl **'indæk** kharīta lil **torok** fī **hǣzihi** æl **mantika**
Where are the toilets?	أين التواليت ؟	æynæl twælit

Asking the way—Street directions

Excuse me.	من فضلك !	min **fad**lak
Can you tell me the way to...?	ما هو الطريق الى ... ؟	mǣ **howæ** æl **tarīk** 'ilǣ
How do I get to...?	كيف أصل الى ... ؟	**kæyfæ** 'asil 'ilǣ
Where does this road lead to?	الى أين يؤدى هذا الطريق ؟	'ilæ 'æynæ yo'æddi **hǣzæ** æl **tarīk**
Can you show me on this map where I am?	من فضلك اشر لى على مكانى على الخريطة .	min **fad**lak 'æshir li 'ælǣ mæ**kǣ**ni 'ælæl kharīta
How far is it to... from here?	ما هى المسافة الى ...	mǣ **hiyæ** æl mæ**sǣ**fæ 'ilǣ

CAR—SERVICE STATION

Miles into kilometres

1 mile = 1.609 kilometres (km)

miles	10	20	30	40	50	60	70	80	90	100
km	16	32	48	64	80	97	113	129	145	161

Kilometres into miles

1 kilometre (km) = 0.62 miles

km	10	20	30	40	50	60	70	80	90	100	110	120	130
miles	6	12	19	25	31	37	44	50	56	62	68	75	81

انك على طريق غلط .	You're on the wrong road.
أذهب الى الأمام .	Go straight ahead.
انه هناك على الشمال (اليمين) .	It's down there on the left (right).
اذهب من هذا الطريق ...	Go that way.
اذهب الى أول (ثانى) تقاطع .	Go to the first (second) crossroads.
انحن الى الشمال (اليمين) عند الاشارة .	Turn left (right) at the traffic lights.

In the rest of this section we'll be more closely concerned with the car itself. We've divided it into two parts:

Part A contains general advice on motoring in the Middle East. It's essentially for reference and is therefore to be browsed over, preferably in advance.

Part B is concerned with the practical details of accidents and breakdown. It includes a list of car parts and a list of things that may go wrong with them. Just show it to the garage mechanic and have him point to the items required.

Part A

Customs—Documentation

Visitors will require the following documents to get their car through customs:

Passport and visa
International driving licence
Car registration papers (log book)*
Tryptic (customs pass booklet for vehicle); not required in Lebanon if you are travelling on a tourist visa

Insurance requirements vary from country to country:

Egypt requires that tourists obtain insurance in order to drive in the country. The International Motor Insurance Certificate (Green Card) is recognized only if Egypt is specifically mentioned on the document. If you haven't taken out an insurance extension before leaving home, you can get coverage at your arrival point in Egypt or through the Egyptian Touring Club Association.

Lebanon has no compulsory insurance requirements, but the Green Card is recognized provided Lebanon is specifically mentioned on the document. Insurance can also be obtained upon arrival through an insurance company in Beirut.

Jordan has no compulsory insurance requirements. It would be advisable, before leaving home, to have your regular insurance policy extended to cover travel in the Middle East. However, coverage can also be obtained locally if needed be.

Though the above information is up to date as we go to press, it is advisable to check with your automobile association or the appropriate consulate before you leave home.

* Egypt requires an international car registration document, obtainable through your local automobile association.

Here's my…	هذا / هذه …	hǣzæ/hǣzihi
driving licence	رخصة القيادة	rokhsit ælkiyǣdæ
insurance policy	بوليصة التامين	bolīsit æltæ'mīn
green card	بوليصة التأمين الدولية	bolīsit æltæ'mīn ældæwliyyæ
passport	باسبوری	paspōri
I haven't anything to declare.	ليس عندى أى شىء أعلن عنه .	læysæ 'indi 'æyy shē' 'oolin 'ænho
I've…	عندى …	'indi
a carton of cigarettes	خرطوشة سجاير	khartūshit sægǣyir
a bottle of whisky	زجاجة وسكى	zogǣgit wiski
a bottle of wine	زجاجة نبيت	zogǣgit nibīt
We're staying for…	سنبقى …	sænabkā
a week	أسبوع	'osbū'
2 weeks*	أسبوعين	'osbūēn
a month	شهر	shahr

Roads

Roads—especially main highways—in the Arab countries are generally good and road signs are usually given in English. We recommend prudent driving until you're familiar with the roads, signs and the driving habits of the local drivers. You'll find that drivers make extensive use of their horns. Don't let this scare you; just be sure to follow the traffic rules.

Pedestrian crossings are marked by white zebra stripes, but the security they seem to offer is often illusory.

Distances are marked in kilometres, and the main highways have road signs. There are rest areas *(isteraha)* at frequent intervals where you can refuel, check your car or make minor repairs while having a drink or snack.

* see grammar

Arab highways are not fenced, and night driving at high speed is dangerous, particularly on desert roads between Alexandria and Cairo where you may unconsciously stray into the desert unless you are alert to the road verge markings.

Speed limits in Arabic countries are as follows:

	Residential areas	Open highways
cars	50 km/h (30 mph)	90 km/h (56 mph)
motorcycles	40 km/h (25 mph)	70 km/h (44 mph)

Parking

Use your common sense when parking. The police are normally reasonably lenient with tourists, but don't push your luck too far. You can be fined on the spot for traffic offenses.

In Egypt, in addition to parking meters, you'll find car parks, where a versatile attendant will park your car for you, if necessary by moving other cars to create a space. He may ask you to leave your handbrake off to facilitate his work of shuffling cars around. You'll recognize him by his special badge. It's customary to give the attendant a small tip for his services.

Excuse me. May I park here?	ممكن أركن [أصف] هنا من فضلك ؟	**mom**kin 'ærkin ['**asiff**] **honǣ** min **fad**lak
How long may I park here?	ما مدة الركن [الصف] المسموحة ؟	mǣ **moddit** æl rækn [æl saff] æl mæsm**ūḥ**æ
What's the charge for parking here?	بكم الركن [الصف] هنا ؟	bi**kæm** æl rækn [æl saff] **honǣ**
Must I leave my lights on?	هل يجب أن أترك النور ؟	hæl **yæ**gib 'æn '**æ**trok æl **nūr**

Road signs

You'll find that many of the standard international road signs are used in the Arab countries. Some special ones are shown on pages 160–161.

Here are some of the main written signs you're likely to encounter when driving in the Middle East.

الطريق يضيق	Road narrows
احترس	Caution
احترس ، أطفال	Attention, children
الزم اليمين	Keep right
تحويلة	Diversion (Detour)
خطر	Danger
طريق منزلق	Slippery road
طريق سريع	Motorway (Expressway)
عبور مشاة	Pedestrians
مزلقان	Level-crossing (Railroad crossing)
قف	Stop
ممنوع الانتظار	No parking
ممنوع الدخول	No entry
مستشفى	Hospital
منحنى خطر	Dangerous bend (curve)
ممنوع تخطى السيارة التى أمامك	No overtaking (No passing)
موقف سيارات	Parking
مدرسة	School
منطقة عمل	Road works (Men working)
هدوء	Silence
شارع اتجاه واحد	One-way street
هدىء السرعة	Slow
هدىء السرعة	Drive slowly

FOR ROAD SIGNS, see also pages 160–161

Part B

Accidents

This section is confined to immediate aid. The legal problems of responsibility and settlement can be taken care of at a later stage. Your first concern will be for the injured.

Is anyone hurt?	هل أصيب أحد ؟	hæl osībæ 'æḥæd
Don't move.	لا تتحرك .	læ tætæḥarrak
It's all right. Don't worry.	لا تقلق . كل شيء على ما يرام .	læ tæ'læ'. kol shē' 'ælæ mæ yorām
Where's the nearest telephone?	أين أقرب تليفون ؟	æynæ 'akrab tilifōn
Can I use your telephone? There's been an accident.	هل يمكنني استعمال تليفونك ؟ فيه حادثه .	hæl yomkinonī 'istiimæl tilifōnæk? fih ḥædsæ
Call a doctor/ambulance quickly.	اطلب دكتور / سيارة اسعاف بسرعة .	otlob doktōr/sæyyārit 'isææf bisoraa
There are people injured.	هناك مصابون .	honæk mosābūn
Help me get them out of the car.	ساعدني على اخراجهم من السيارة .	sæ'idni 'ælæ 'ikhrāgihim min æl sæyyāra

Police—Exchange of information

Please call the police.	من فضلك اطلب البوليس .	min fadlak 'otlob æl bolīs
There's been an accident. It's about 3 kilometres from...	لقد وقع حادث على بعد ٣ كيلومتر من ...	lakad wakaa ḥædis 'ælæ bood 3 kilomitr min
I'm on the Cairo–Alexandria road, 25 kilometres from Alexandria.	أنا على طريق مصر – اسكندرية على بعد ٢٥ كيلومتر من الاسكندرية .	'ænæ ælæ tarīk masr–'iskindiriyyæ 'ælæ bood 25 kilomitr minæl 'iskændæriyyæ
Here's my name and address.	هذا اسمي وعنواني .	hæzæ 'ismi wæ 'innæni

Would you mind acting as a witness?	هل يمكنك أن تشهد ؟	hæl yomkinæk 'æn tæshhæd
I'd like an interpreter.	أريد مترجم .	orid motærgim

Remember to put out a red triangle warning if the car is out of action or impeding traffic.

Breakdown

...and that's what we'll do with this section: break it down into four phases.

1. *On the road*
   You ask where the nearest garage is.
2. *At the garage*
   You tell the mechanic what's wrong.
3. *Finding the trouble*
   He tells you what he thinks is wrong.
4. *Getting it fixed*
   You tell him to fix it and, once that's done, settle the account (or argue about it).

Phase 1—On the road

Where's the nearest garage?	أين أقرب جراج ؟	æynæ 'akrab garāzh
Excuse me. My car has broken down. May I use your phone?	سيارتى تعطلت . هل يمكنني استخدام تليفـونك من فضلك ؟	sæyyārati ta'attalat. hæl yomkinoni 'istikhdæm tilifōnæk min fadlak
What's the telephone number of the nearest garage?	ما نمرة تليفون أقرب جراج ؟	mæ nimrit tilifōn akrab garāzh
I've had a breakdown at...	تعطلت سيارتى عند ...	ta'attalat sæyyārati 'indæ

We are on the Beirut–Tripoli road, about 10 kilometres from Beirut.	نحن على طريق بيروت – طرابلس ، على بعد ١٠ كم من بيروت .	næḥno ælǣ tarīk bæyrūt–tarablos ælǣ bood ashara kilomitr min bæyrūt
Can you send a mechanic?	من فضلك ارسل لنـا ميكانيكى .	min fadlak arsil lænǣ mikænīki
Can you send a truck to tow my car?	من فضلك ارسل لنا لورى لسحب السيارة .	min fadlak arsil lænǣ lōri lisæḥb ælsayyāra
How long will you be?	متى ترجع ؟	mætǣ targaa

Phase 2—At the garage

Can you help me?	هل يمكنك مساعدتى ؟	hæl yomkinæk mosǣ'ædæti
I don't know what's wrong with it.	لا أعرف ما بها .	lǣ aaraf mǣ bihǣ
I think there's something wrong with the…	أظن أن … به عيب .	azonn ænnæ… bihi ēb
axle	محور العجلة	miḥwar æl 'ægælæ
battery	البطارية	æl battariyya
brakes	الفرامل	æl farāmil
clutch	الدبرياج	æl dibriyǣzh
contact	الكونتاكت	æl kontækt
dip (dimmer) switch	مفتاح النور	moftǣḥ æl nūr
direction indicator	الاشارة	æl 'ishāra
door	البـاب	æl bǣb
dynamo	الدينامو	æl dinamō
electrical system	الكهرباء	æl kahraba
engine	الموتور	æl motōr
fuel feed	خرطوم البنزين	khartūm æl bænzīn
gears	التروس	æl torūs
generator	الدينامو	æl dinæmō
horn	آلة التنبيه [الكلاكسون]	'ǣlæt æl tænbih [klækson]
ignition system	المـارش	æl marsh

CAR—REPAIRS

lights	النور	æl 'adwā'
brake lights	نور الفرامل	nūr æl farāmil
headlights	النور الأمامى	æl nūr æl 'æmǣmi
rear (tail) lights	النور الخلفى	æl nūr æl **khælfi**
reversing (backup) lights	نور السير للخلف	nūr æl marsh **khælfi**
muffler	ماسورة العادم [الشكمان]	masūrit æl ādim [æl shæk**mǣn**]
oil system	الزيت	æl zēt
radiator	الرادياتير	æl radia**tēr**
seat	الكرسى	æl **korsi**
silencer	ماسورة العادم [الشكمان]	masūrit æl ādim [æl shæk**mǣn**]
speedometer	عداد السرعة	æd**dǣd** æl **soraa**
starter motor	الاستارتر [المارش]	æl 'istartir [æl marsh]
steering	عجلة القيادة [الدركسيون]	æ**gæ**lit æl ki**yā**dæ [æl dirik**syōn**]
suspension	السوست [السسبنسيون]	æl **so**sæt [æl sospæn**syōn**]
transmission	عمود الكردان	æ**mūd** ælkir**dǣn**
turn signal	الاشارة	æl 'i**shā**ra
wheels	العجل [الدواليب]	æl **æ**gæl [æl dwa**līb**]
wipers	المساحات	æl mæssæ**ḥǣt**

LEFT	RIGHT
يسار	يمين
(yæsār)	(yæmīn)

FRONT	BACK
أمـام	خلف
('æmǣm)	(khælf)

It's (too) ...	انه ...	innæho
backfiring	يصفق	yo**saf**fik
bad	سيىء	**sæ**yyi'
blown	ضارب	**dā**rib
broken	مكسور	mak**sūr**
burnt	محترق	**moḥ**tarik
chafing	يحتك	yæḥ**tækk**
cracked	مشقوق	mæsh**kūk**

defective	بـايظ	bāyiz
disconnected	غير واصل	gēr wāsil
dry	جـاف	gæff
jammed	مزنوق	mæznū'
jerking	يخبط	yokhabbitt
knocking	يدق	yædok
leaking	يخر	yækhorr
loose	مفكوك	mæfkūk
noisy	يسبب صوتاً	yosæbbib sawtan
overheating	يسبب سخونة شديدة	yosæbbib sokhūnæ shædīdæ
slack	غير مشدود	gēr mæshdūd
slipping	ينزلق [يزحط]	yænzalik [yozaḥḥit]
split	منقسم	monkasim
stuck	مزنوق	mæznū'
vibrating	يهتز	yæhtæzz
weak	ضعيف	da'īf
The car won't start.	السيارة لا تدور .	æl sayyāra lā tadūr
The car won't pull.	السيارة لا تسحب .	æl sayyāra lā tæsḥæb
The car is making a funny noise.	السيارة بها صوت غريب .	æl sayyāra bihæ sōt gærīb
It's locked and the keys are inside.	السيارة مقفولة والمفتاح بداخلها .	æl sayyāra mæskūkæ wæl moftæḥ bidækhilhæ
The radiator is leaking.	الرادياتير يخر .	æl radyatēr yækhorr
The clutch engages too quickly.	الدبرياج يفلت بسرعة .	æl dibriyæzh yæflit bisoraa
The steering wheel's vibrating.	عجلة القيادة تهتز .	'ægælit æl kiyāda tæhtæzz
The suspension is weak.	السوست [السسبنسيون] ضعيفة .	æl sosætt [æl sospænsyōn] da'īfa
The ... needs adjusting.	الـ... محتاج الى ضبط .	æl... moḥtæg ilæ dabt
brake/clutch/idling	فرامل/دبرياج/سيلانسيه	farāmil/dibriyæzh/silansyēh

Now that you've explained what's wrong, you'll want to know how long it will take to repair it and arrange yourself accordingly.

How long will it take to repair?	ما مدة التصليح ؟	mææ tūl moddæt æl taslīḥ
Suppose I come back tomorrow?	هل أرجع بكرة ؟	hæl argaa bokra
Can you give me a lift into town?	هل يمكنك توصيلى الى المدينة ؟	hæl yomkinæk tawsīli ilææ ælmædīnæ
Is there a place to stay nearby?	هل يوجد مكان قريب للبقاء فيه ؟	hæl yūgæd mækææn karīb lil bakā' fīh

Phase 3—Finding the trouble

It's up to the mechanic either to find the trouble or to repair it. All you have to do is hand him the book and point to the text in Arabic below.

من فضلك راجع القــائمة التالية وأشر الى ما به عيب . واذا أراد الزبون معرفة العيب بالضبط فابحث عن اللفظ المنــاسب فى القائمة التى تليهــا (مكسور ، به ماس كهربائى ، الخ . .) *

فلتر الهواء	air filter
البطارية	battery
البيلاّت	bearing
علبة السلندرات	block
قفــل	bolt
الفرامل	brake
اسطوانة الفرامل [الطمبور]	brake drum
تيل الفرامل [الكولييه]	brake lining
جهاز هيدروليكية الفرامل	brake hydraulic system

* Please look at the following alphabetical list and point to the defective item. If your customer wants to know exactly what's wrong with it, pick the applicable term from the next list (broken, short-circuited, etc.).

brushes	الفرش
cable	الكابل
crankshaft	عمود الكامة
carburettor	الكاربراتير
casing	قميص السلندر
choke	الهواء
chassis	الشاسيه
clutch	الدبرياج
clutch plate	اسطوانة الدبرياج
coil	البوبينة
condenser	الكوندنسر
connecting (piston) rod	عمود اتصال البستم
connection	التوصيلة
contact	الكونتاكت
cooling system	جهاز التبريد
crankshaft	البيلاّت
crown wheel and pinion	الكورونة والترس
cylinder	السلندر
cylinder head	وجه السلندرات
cylinder head gasket	جوان السلندرات
diaphragm	الغشاء
differential	الدفرنسيال
distributor	الدستربيوتر
distributor leads	أسلاك الدستربيوتر
dynamo (generator)	الدينامو
electrical system	كهرباء السيارة
engine	الموتور
fan belt	سير المروحة
filter	الفلتر
float	العوامة
flywheel	عجلة القيادة [الدركسيون]
fuel gauge/pump/feed/tank	عداد/طلمبة/خرطوم/خزان البنزين
gauge	العداد

علبة التروس	gear box
الإشعال	ignition coil
جوان	joint (packing)
الأسلاك	leads
العمود الرئيسى	main bearing
ماسورة العادم [الشكمان]	manifold
الخليط [الكاربراتير]	mixture
قواعد الموتور	mountings
تبريد/فلتر/طلمبة الزيت	oil cooler/filter/pump
البستم	piston
أماكن الاتصال	points
الطلمبة	pump
الرادياتير	radiator
الرباط	relay
السجمان – حول البستم	rings
شاكوش الدستربيوتر	rotor arm
عمود	shaft
الأمرتسير	shock-absorber
ماسك الفرامل	shoes
ماسورة العادم	silencer (muffler)
البوجيهات	sparking plugs
السوستة [الرفّاص]	spring
بوبينة المارش	starter armature
المارش	starter motor
عجلة القيادة	steering
علبة عجلة القيادة	steering box
السوست [الرفّاصات]	suspension
القلّاب	tappet
الأسنان	teeth
الترموستات	thermostat
توقيت الكهرباء	timing
زوايا العجل	tracking
عمود الكردان	transmission

جوان الكردان	universal joint
البلف [السوباب]	valve
طلمبة الماء	water pump
العجل [الدواليب]	wheels
الأسلاك	wiring

بالقائمة التالية بها كلمات تدل على العيب الموجود فى السيارة أو ما يلزم عمله. *

ضبط	to adjust
ضبط الاتزان	to balance
تفريغ	to bleed
مفرقع	blown
مكسور	broken
محترق	burnt
تغيير	to change
شحن	to charge
تنظيف	to clean
به صدأ – متآكل	corroded
مشقوق	cracked
عطلان	defective
وسخ	dirty
غير واصل	disconnected
جاف	dry
خرط الصبابات	to grind in
عالى	high
مزنوق	jammed
يغر	leaking
مفكوك	loose
فك	to loosen
منخفض	low
يقطّع [الموتور]	misfiring

* The following list contains words about what's wrong or what may need to be done with the car.

لا يشحن	not charging
يسخن بشدة	overheating
متآكل	pitted
لعب	play
سريع	quick
تغيير التيلة	to reline
استبدال – تغيير	to replace
الخليط غنى فى الكابراتير	rich
به ماس كهربائى	short-circuited
غير مشدود	slack
ينزلق [يزحط]	slipping
فك الموتور	to strip down
احكام الربط	to tighten
ضعيف	weak
متآكل	worn

Phase 4—Getting it repaired

Have you found the trouble?	هل وجدت العيب ؟	hæl wæ**gædt** æl ēb
Is that serious?	هل هو أمر خطير ؟	hæl **howæ** **am**ron khatīr
Can you repair it?	هل يمكنك اصلاحها ؟	hæl yom**kin**æk islā**ḥ**æhǣ
Can you do it now?	هل يمكنك اصلاحها الآن ؟	hæl yom**kin**æk islā**ḥ**æhǣ æl ʼ**ǣn**
What's it going to cost?	كم ستتكلف ؟	kæm sætætæ**kæl**læf

What if he says "no"?

Why can't you do it?	لماذا لا يمكنك اصلاحها ؟	li**mǣ**zæ lǣ yom**kin**æk islā**ḥ**æha
Is it essential to have that part?	هل هذه القطعة ضرورية ؟	hæl **hǣ**zihi æl **ki**taa darū**riy**ya

How long is it going to take to get the spare parts?	متى يمكن الحصول على قطع الغيار ؟	**mæt**ǣ **yom**kin æl ḥosūl ælǣ kitaa æl giyār
Where's the nearest garage that can repair it?	أين أقرب جراج يمكنه اصلاحها ؟	æynæ **akrab garāzh** yom**kinoho** islāḥæhæ
Can you fix it so that I can get as far as...?	هل يمكنك اصلاحها حتى أصل الى ...	hæl yom**kin**æk islāḥæhæ ḥættǣ asill ilǣ

If you're really stuck, ask:

Can I leave my car here for a day/a few days?	هل أستطيع أن أترك سيارتى هنا لمدة يوم / بضعة أيام ؟	hæl astatī æn **atrok** sayya**rati** **hon**ǣ **limod**dæt yōm/**bidaat** æyy**ǣm**

Settling the bill

Is everything fixed?	هل تم اصلاح كل شيء ؟	hæl **tæm**mæ isla**ḥ** koll shē'
How much do I owe you?	كم الحساب ؟	kæm æl ḥis**ǣb**
Will you take a traveller's cheque?	هل تقبل الشيكات السياحية ؟	hæl **tak**bæl æl shik**ǣt** æl siy**ǣḥ**iyyæ
Thanks very much for your help.	شكراً جزيلا على مساعدتك.	**shok**ran gæzilæn ælǣ mosǣ'ædatikæ
This is for you.	هذا لك .	h**ǣ**zæ læk

But you may feel that the workmanship is sloppy or that you're paying for work not done. Get the bill itemized. If necessary, get it translated before you pay.

I'd like to check the bill first. Will you itemize the work done?	أريد مراجعة الحساب . من فضلك اكتب تفصيل الشغل .	orīd morag'it æl ḥis**ǣ**b. min **fad**lak **iktib** taf**sīl** æl shogl

If the garage still won't back down–and you're sure you're right—get the help of a third party.

Some Arabic road signs

No U turn

No left turn

No entry

No right turn

Maximum load 10 tons

Maximum speed 60 kph.

Maximum height 4 m.

Maximum width 2 m.

No stopping

Road closed

Parking

No parking

Hospital

No honking

Animal-drawn vehicles prohibited

Handcarts prohibited

اتجاه اجبارى
One way

محطة بنزين
Petrol

ورشة تصليح
Garage

مركز اسعاف ونجدة
First-aid post

مزلقان مفتوح
vel (railroad) crossing without barrier

أقصى عرض
Maximum width 3 m.

أقصى ارتفاع
Maximum height 4 m.

كوبرى متحرك
Opening or swing bridge

مطب
Dip

طريق غير مستو
Uneven road

طريق متعرّج.
Winding road

منحدر خطر
Steep hill

أمامك علامة قف
Stop at major road ahead

تقاطع الطريق
Side road

علامة
سانت أندروز
(مزلقان سكك حديد)
Location of level (railroad) crossing without gate or barrier

Doctor

Frankly, how much use is a phrase book going to be to you in the case of serious injury or illness? The only phrase you need in such an emergency is...

Get a doctor—quick!	اطلب دكتور – بسرعة !	**ot**lob dok**tōr**—bi**so**raa

But there are minor aches and pains, ailments and irritations that can upset the best planned trip. Here we can help you—and, perhaps, the doctor.

Many doctors will speak English well; others will know enough for your needs. But suppose there's something the doctor can't explain because of language difficulties? We've thought of that. As you'll see, this section has been arranged to enable you and the doctor to communicate. From page 165 to 171, you'll find your side of the dialogue on the upper half of each page; the doctor's is on the lower half.

The whole section has been divided into three parts: illness, wounds, nervous tension. Page 171 is concerned with prescriptions and fees.

General

Can you get me a doctor?	اطلب لى دكتور من فضلك.	**ot**lob li dok**tōr** min **fad**lak
Is there a doctor here?	هل يوجد دكتور هنا ؟	hæl **yū**gæd dok**tōr** **ho**næ
Where's there a doctor who speaks English?	أين يوجد دكتور يتكلم انجليزى ؟	æynæ **yū**gæd dok**tōr** yætæ**kæl**læm ingi**lī**zi
Where's the surgery (doctor's office)?	أين مكتب الدكتور ؟	æynæ **mæk**tæb æl dok**tōr**
What are the surgery (office) hours?	ما هى مواعد العيادة ؟	mææ **hi**yæ mæwæ**ïd** æl 'i**yææ**dæ

Could the doctor come to see me here?	هل يستطيع الدكتور الكشف علىّ هنا ؟	hæl yastatī æl doktōr æl kæshf allayya honā
What time can the doctor come?	متى يستطيع الدكتور الحضور ؟	mætǣ yastatī æl doktōr æl ḥodūr

Symptoms

Use this section to tell the doctor what's wrong. Basically, what he'll need to know is:

What? (ache, pain, bruise, etc.)
Where? (arm, stomach, etc.)
How long? (have you had the trouble)

Before you visit the doctor find out the answers to these questions by glancing through the pages that follow.

Parts of the body

ankle	قصبة الرجل	kasabit æl rigl
appendix	المصران الأعور	æl mosrān æl 'aawar
arm	ذراع	zirāa
artery	شريان	shoryææn
back	ظهر	zahr
bladder	مثانة	mæsæænæ
blood	دم	dæmm
bone	عظم	azm
breast	ثدى	sædy
chest	صدر	sadr
collar-bone	الترقوة	æl torkowæ
ear	أذن	'ozon
elbow	كوع	kū'
eye	عين	ēn
finger	أصبع	asbaa

foot	قدم	kadam
gland	غدة	goddæ
hand	يد	yædd
head	رأس	ra's
heart	قلب	kalb
heel	كعب	kææb
hip	ردف	rædf
intestines	مصارين	masarin
joint	مفصل	mifsal
kidney	كلية	kilyæ
knee/knee cap	ركبة / صابونة الركبة	rokbæ/sabūnit æl rokbæ
leg	ساق	sæk
liver	كبد	kæbid
lung	رئة	ri'æ
mouth	فم	fæm
muscle	عضل	'adal
neck	رقبة	rakabæ
nerve	عصب	'asab
nervous system	الجهاز العصبى	æl gihææz æl'asabi
nose	أنف	ænf
rib	ضلع	dil'
shoulder	كتف	kitf
skin	الجلد	æl gild
spine	العمود الفقرى	æl 'æmūd æl fakri
stomach	المعدة	æl mi'idæ
tendon	العرقوب	æl 'orkūb
throat	الزور [الزلاعيم]	æl zōr [æl zælæ'im]
toe	أصبع القدم	asbaa æl kadam
tongue	لسان	lisææn
tonsils	اللوز	æl liwæzz
urine	بول	bōl
vein	عرق	'irk
wrist	معصم	mi'sam

PATIENT

Part 1—Illness

I'm not feeling well.	لا أشعر أني كويس .	læ **ash'or** ænni **kwæyyis**
I've got a pain here.	عندى ألم هنا .	indi 'ælæm **honæ**
His/Her...hurts.	عنده / عندها ألم فى ال...	indo/indæhæ 'ælæm fil
I've got (a)...	عندى ...	indi
headache/backache	صداع / ألم فى الظهر	sodāa/'ælæm fil dahr
fever/sore throat	حرارة / ألم فى الحلق	ḥarāra/'ælæm fil ḥolok
I'm constipated.	عندى امساك .	indi imsæk
I've been vomiting.	عندى قيء .	indi kē'
I feel...	أشعر ...	ash'or
faint/dizzy	بضعف / بدوخة	bidaaf/bidōkhæ
nauseated/shivery	بصداع / برعشة	bisodāa/biraasha

DOCTOR

الجزء الأول – المرض

ما العلة ؟	What's the trouble?
أين الالم ؟	Where does it hurt?
منذ متى وأنت تشعر بهذا الالم ؟	How long have you had this pain?
منذ متى وأنت تشعر بهذا؟	How long have you been feeling like this?
شمر قميصك من فضلك .	Roll up your sleeve.
اخلع ملابسك (حتى الوسط) .	Please undress (down to the waist).
من فضلك اخلع البنطلون واللباس .	Please remove your trousers and underpants.

PATIENT

I've/He's/She's got (a/an)...	عندى / عنده / عندها...	indi/indo/indæhæ
abscess	دمل	dimmil
asthma	ربو	rabw
boil	خراج	khorrāg
chill	برد	bærd
cold	زكام	zokǣm
constipation	امساك	imsǣk
convulsions	تشنجات	tæshænnogǣt
cramps	شد عضلى	takallosāt
diarrhoea	اسهال	ishǣl
fever	حرارة	harāra
haemorrhoids	بواسير	bæwǣsīr
hay fever	زكام ربيعى	zokǣm rabīi
hernia	فتق	fætk

DOCTOR

ارقد هنا من فضلك .	Please lie down over here.
افتح فمك .	Open your mouth.
تنفس بعمق .	Breathe deeply.
اسعل من فضلك .	Cough, please.
هل هى أول مرة تشعر بهذا ؟	Is this the first time you've had this?
ساقيس درجة حرارتك .	I'll take your temperature.
ساقيص ضغط دمك .	I'm going to take your blood pressure.
سأعطيك حقنة .	I'll give you an injection.
أريد عينة من البول / البراز .	I want a sample of your urine/stools.
سأصف لك مضاد حيوى .	I'll prescribe an antibiotic.

PATIENT

indigestion	عصر هضم	'osr hadm
inflammation of...	التهاب فى ...	'iltihææb fi
influenza	انفلونزا	'ænfilwænzæ
morning sickness	صداع الصباح	sodāa æl sabāḥ
rheumatism	روماتزم	romætizm
stiff neck	التواء فى العنق	'iltiwææ' fil 'onok
sunburn	حرق من الشمس	ḥark min æl shæms
sunstroke	ضربة شمس	darbit shæms
tonsillitis	التهاب فى الزور [الزلاعيم]	'iltihææb fil zōr
ulcer	قرحة	korḥa
whooping cough	سعال ديكى	soææl dīki
It's nothing serious, I hope?	أرجو أن لا يوجد ما يدعو الى القلق .	'argū 'ællæ yūgæd mææ yæd'ū 'ilæl kalak

DOCTOR

لا يوجد ما يدعو الى القلق.	It's nothing to worry about.
عندك ...	You've got (a/an)...
حساسية/ التهاب فى الزور [الزلاعيم]	allergy/angina
التهاب فى الزائدة الدودية/ التهاب فى القصبة الهوائية	appendicitis/bronchitis
التهاب فى المثانة / دسنتريا	cystitis/dysentery
تسمم / الصفراء	food poisoning/jaundice
لمباجو / التهاب رئوى	lumbago/pneumonia
التهاب فى ...	an inflammation of...
يجب أن تذهب الى طبيب متخصص .	I want you to see a specialist.
يجب أن تذهب الى المستشفى لاجراء كشف عام .	I want you to go to the hospital for a general check-up.

PATIENT

I'm a diabetic.	عندى مرض السكر .	indi marad æl **sokkar**
I've a cardiac condition.	أنا مريض بالقلب .	ænæ **marīd** bil kalb
I had a heart attack in…	أصابتنى ذبحة صدرية فى …	asābætni **zæbḥæ** sad**riyya** fi
I'm allergic to…	عندى حساسية ضد …	indi ḥæsæ**siy**yæ didd
I'd like you to prescribe some medicine for me.	اكتب لى دواء من فضلك.	oktob li dæ**wǣ**' min **fad**lak
This is my usual medicine.	هذا هو دوائى المعتاد .	**hǣ**zæ **how**e dæ**wǣ**'i æl**mo'tǣd**
I need this medicine.	أنا محتاج لهذا الدواء .	ænǣ moḥ**tǣg** li **hǣ**zæ æl dæ**wǣ**
I'm expecting a baby.	أنا حامل .	ænǣ **ḥǣ**mil
Can I travel?	هل يمكننى السفر ؟	hæl yom**ki**noni æl **sa**far

DOCTOR

ما كمية الانسولين التى تأخذها ؟	What dose of insulin are you taking?
بحقنة أم بالفم ؟	Injection or oral?
ما العلاج الذى تتبعه ؟	What treatment have you been having?
ما الدواء التى تأخذه ؟	What medicine have you been taking?
عندك ذبحة صدرية (خفيفة) .	You've had a (slight) heart attack.
لا نستعمل … هذا مشابه له جداً .	We don't use… This is very similar.
متى تتوقعين الولادة ؟	When's the baby due?
يجب ألا تسافرى حتى…	You can't travel until…

PATIENT

Part 2—Wounds

Could you have a look at this...?	من فضلك اكشف على هذا / هذه ...	min **fad**lak ikshif ælæ hæzæ/hæzihi
boil	الخراج	æl khorrāg
bruise	الكدمة	æl **kæd**mæ
burn	الحرق	æl ḥark
cut	القطع	æl kat'
graze	خدش	æl khædsh
insect bite	قرصة حشرة	'arsit ḥashara
rash	الطفح	æl tafḥ
swelling	الورم	æl waram
wound	الجرح	æl gærḥ
I can't move my...	لا أستطيع أن أحرك ...	læ astatī æn oḥærrik...
It hurts.	انه يؤلمني .	innæho yo'limoni

DOCTOR

الجزء الثانى – الجروح

انه (ليس) متلوثا .	It's (not) infected.
عندك انزلاق غضروفى .	You've got a slipped disc.
يجب أن تعمل أشعة .	I want you to have an X-ray.
انه ...	It's...
مكسور / ملتوى	broken/sprained
متحرك من مكانه / متمزق	dislocated/torn
سأصف لك مطهر .	I'll give you an antiseptic.
ليس ما يدعو الى القلق .	It's not serious.
أريد أن تأتى لاراك بعد ... يوم .	I want you to come and see me in... days' time.

PATIENT

Part 3—Nervous tension

I'm in a nervous state.	أنا فى حالة عصبية .	ænæ fi **ḥæ**læ asa**biy**ya
I'm feeling depressed.	أشعر باكتئاب .	**ash**'or bi'ikti'**ææ**b
I want some sleeping pills.	أريد حبوبا منومة .	o**rīd** ḥobūbæn monæwwimæ
I can't eat.	لا أستطيع أن آكل .	læ astatī æn **ææ**kol
I can't sleep.	لا أستطيع أن أنام .	læ astatī æn æn**ææ**m
I'm having nightmares.	عندى كوابيس .	**in**di kæwæ**bīs**
Can you prescribe a...?	من فضلك اكتب لى...	min **fad**lak ik**ti**bli
sedative/tranquillizer	مسكن / مهدىء	mo**sæk**kin/mo**hæd**di'
anti-depressant	مضاد للاكتئاب	mo**dād** lil'ikti'**ææ**b

DOCTOR

الجزء الثالث – التوتر العصبى

عندك اجهاد عصبى .	You're suffering from nervous tension.
انت محتاج الى راحة .	You need a rest.
ما الاقراص التى تتناولها ؟	What pills have you been taking?
كم قرص فى اليوم ؟	How many a day?
منذ متى وأنت تشعر بهذا ؟	How long have you been feeling like this?
سأصف لك بعض الاقراص	I'll prescribe some pills.
سأصف لك مسكنا .	I'll give you a sedative.

PATIENT

Prescriptions and dosage

What kind of medicine is this?	ما نوع هذا الدواء ؟	mǣ nōo hǣzæ ældæwǣ'
How many times a day should I take it?	كم مرة فى اليوم يجب أن أتناوله ؟	kæm marra fil yōm yægib æn ætænǣwælho
Must I swallow them whole?	هل أبتلعها كاملة ؟	hæl æbtæli'hǣ kǣmilæ

Fee

How much do I owe you?	كم يجب أن أدفع لك ؟	kæm yægib æn ædfææ læk
Do I pay you now or will you send me your bill?	هل أدفع لك الآن أم سترسل لى الحساب ؟	hæl ædfææ læk æl'ǣn æm sætorsil li ælḥisǣb
Thanks for your help, doctor.	شكراً على مساعدتك يادكتور .	shokran ælǣ mosǣ'ædætikæ yǣ doktōr

---

DOCTOR

الجزء الرابع – العلاج والجرعة

خذ ... ملعقة شاى من هذا الدواء كل ... ساعة .	Take... teaspoon(s) of this medicine every ... hours.
خذ ... قرص مع كوب ماء ...	Take... tablets with a glass of water...
. . . مرة فى اليوم	...times a day
قبل الطعام / بعد الطعام	before each meal/after each meal
فى الصباح / فى المساء	in the mornings/at night

الحساب

الحساب ... من فضلك .	That's... please.
من فضلك ادفع الآن .	Please pay me now.
سأرسل لك الحساب .	I'll send you a bill.

Dentist

Can you recommend a good dentist?	من فضلك انصحنى بطبيب أسنان جيد .	min **fadlak** insaḥni bitabīb æsnǣn gæyyid
Can I make an (urgent) appointment to see Dr.... ?	أريد موعداً (عاجلا) مع الدكتور ...	orīd maw'idæn ('ǣgilæn) maal doktōr
Can't you possibly make it earlier than that?	ألا يمكن أن يكون الموعد قبل ذلك ؟	'ælǣ **yomkin** æn yækūn æl **maw'id** kabl **zǣlik**
I've a toothache.	عندى ألم فى أسنانى .	indi 'ælæm fi æs**nǣ**ni
I've an abscess.	عندى خراج .	indi khor**rāg**
This tooth hurts.	هذه السنة تؤلمنى .	hǣzihi æl **sin**næ to'limoni
at the top	الى أعلى [فوق]	ilǣ 'æælǣ [fōk]
at the bottom	الى أسفل [تحت]	ilǣ æsfæl [tæḥt]
in the front	الى الامام	ilǣ æl 'æ**mǣm**
at the back	الى الخلف	ilǣ æl khælf
Can you fix it temporarily?	هل يمكنك علاجها مؤقتاً ؟	hæl yom**kin**æk ilǣgæhǣ mo'akkatæn
I don't want it extracted.	لا أريد خلعها .	lǣ orīd khæl'ihǣ
I've lost a filling.	سقط حشو السنة .	sakata ḥæshw æl **sin**næ
The gum is...	اللثة ...	æl læsæ
very sore	تؤلمنى بشدة	to' limoni bi**shid**dæ
bleeding	تنزف	tænzif

Dentures

I've broken this denture.	كسرت هذا الطقم .	kasart **hǣ**zæ æl takm
Can you repair this denture?	هل يمكنك اصلاح هذا الطقم ؟	hæl yom**kin**æk is**lāḥ** **hǣ**zæ æl **takm**
When will it be ready?	متى يكون جاهزاً ؟	mætǣ yækūn gǣhizæn

Optician

I've broken my glasses.	كسرت نظارتى [عويناتى] .	kasart nazzārati ['owæynǣti]
Can you repair them for me?	هل يمكنك اصلاحها ؟	hæl yomkinæk islāḫæhæ
When will they be ready?	متى تكون جاهزة ؟	mætǣ tækūn gǣhizæ
Can you change the lenses?	هل يمكنك تغيير العدسة؟	hæl yomkinæk tæg̣yīr æl 'ædæsæ
I want tinted lenses.	أريد عدسة غامقة .	orīd 'ædæsæ g̣ǣmika
I want contact lenses.	أريد عدسات لاصقة .	orīd ædæsǣt lāsika
I'd like to buy a pair of sunglasses.	أريد شراء نظارة شمس.	orīd shirā' nazzārit shæms
I'd like to buy a pair of binoculars.	أريد شراء نظارة معظمة.	orīd shirā' nazzara mo'azzima
How much do I owe you?	كم الحساب ؟	kæm æl ḥisǣb
Do I pay you now or will you send me your bill?	هل أدفع لك الآن . أم سترسل لى الفاتورة ؟	hæl ædfæ læk æl'ǣn æm sætorsil lī æl fatūra

FOR NUMBERS, see page 175

Reference section

Where do you come from?

Africa	افريقيا	æfrīka
Algeria	الجزائر	æl gæzæ'ir
Asia	آسيا	'æsyæ
Australia	استراليا	ostralyā
Canada	كندا	kænædæ
Egypt	مصر	misr
Europe	أوروبا	orobba
France	فرنسا	faransa
Great Britain	انجلترا	ingiltirā
Greece	اليونان	æl yonæn
Ireland	ايرلندا	irlanda
Italy	ايطاليا	italyā
India	الهند	æl hind
Iraq	العراق	æl 'irāk
Jordan	الاردن	æl 'ordon
Lebanon	لبنان	libnæn
Libya	ليبيا	libyæ
Middle East	الشرق الاوسط	æl shark æl 'awsat
Morocco	المغرب [مراكش]	æl mægrib [marākish]
New Zealand	نيوزيلندا	nyū zilændæ
North America	أمريكا الشمالية	æmrīkæ æl shæmæliyyæ
Saudi Arabia	السعودية	æl so'ūdiyyæ
South Africa	جنوب افريقيا	gænūb afrikyā
South America	أمريكا الجنوبية	æmrīkæ æl gænūbiyyæ
Sudan	السودان	æl sūdæn
Syria	سوريا	sūriyyæ
Tunisia	تونس	tūnis
Turkey	تركيا	torkiyæ
USA	الولايات المتحدة	æl wilæyæt æl mottæḥidæ
USSR	روسيا	rosyæ

Numbers

٠	0	صفر	sifr
١	1	واحد	wǣḥid
٢	2	اثنين	′itnēn
٣	3	ثلاثة	tælǣtæ
٤	4	أربعة	arbaa
٥	5	خمسة	khæmsæ
٦	6	ستة	sittæ
٧	7	سبعة	sæb′æ
٨	8	ثمانية	tæmǣnyæ
٩	9	تسعة	tisaa
١٠	10	عشرة	ashara
١١	11	أحد عشرة	ḥidāshar
١٢	12	اثنى عشر	itnāshar
١٣	13	ثلاثة عشر	talattāshar
١٤	14	أربعة عشر	arbaatāshar
١٥	15	خمسة عشر	khamastāshar
١٦	16	ستة عشر	sittāshar
١٧	17	سبعة عشر	sabaatāshar
١٨	18	ثمانية عشر	tamantāshar
١٩	19	تسعة عشر	tisaatāshar
٢٠	20	عشرين	′ishrīn
٢١	21	واحد وعشرين	wǣḥid wæ ′ishrīn
٢٢	22	اثنين وعشرين	′itnēn wæ ′ishrīn
٢٣	23	ثلاثة وعشرين	tælǣtæ wæ ′ishrīn
٢٤	24	أربعة وعشرين	arbaa wa ′ishrīn
٢٥	25	خمسة وعشرين	khæmsæ wæ ′ishrīn
٢٦	26	ستة وعشرين	sittæ wæ ′ishrīn
٢٧	27	سبعة وعشرين	sæb′a wæ ′ishrīn
٢٨	28	ثمانية وعشرين	tæmænyæ wæ ′ishrīn
٢٩	29	تسعة وعشرين	tisaa wæ ′ishrīn
٣٠	30	ثلاثين	tælætīn
٣١	31	واحد وثلاثين	wǣḥid wæ tælætīn

٣٢	32	اثنين وثلاثين	'itnēn wæ tælætīn
٤٠	40	أربعين	ærbi'īn
٥٠	50	خمسين	khæmsīn
٦٠	60	ستين	sittīn
٧٠	70	سبعين	sæb'īn
٨٠	80	ثمانين	tæmænīn
٩٠	90	تسعين	tis'īn
١٠٠	100	مائة	miyyæ
١٠١	101	مائة وواحد	miyyæ wæ wǣhid
١١٠	110	مائة وعشرة	miyyæ wæ ashara
١٢٠	120	مائة وعشرين	miyyæ wæ ishrīn
١٥٠	150	مائة وخمسين	miyyæ wæ khæmsīn
١٦٠	160	مائة وستين	miyyæ wæ sittīn
١٧٠	170	مائة وسبعين	miyyæ wæ sæb'īn
١٨٠	180	مائة وثمانين	miyyæ wæ tæmænīn
١٩٠	190	مائة وتسعين	miyyæ wæ tis'īn
٢٠٠	200	مائتين	mitēn
٣٠٠	300	ثلاثمائة	toltomiyyæ
٤٠٠	400	أربعمائة	rob'omiyyæ
٥٠٠	500	خمسمائة	khomsomiyyæ
٦٠٠	600	ستمائة	sittomiyyæ
٧٠٠	700	سبعمائة	sob'omiyyæ
٨٠٠	800	ثمانمائة	tomnomiyyæ
٩٠٠	900	تسعمائة	tos'omiyyæ
١٠٠٠	1,000	ألف	'ælf
١١٠٠	1,100	ألف ومائة	'ælf wæ miyyæ
٥,٠٠٠	5,000	خمسة آلاف	khæmsæt 'ǣlǣf
١٠,٠٠٠	10,000	عشرة آلاف	asharat 'ǣlǣf
١٠٠,٠٠٠	100,000	مائة ألف	mīt 'ælf
١,٠٠٠,٠٠٠	1,000,000	مليون	milyōn

first	أول	'æwwæl
second	ثانى	tǣni
third	ثالث	tǣlit
fourth	رابع	rābi'
fifth	خامس	khǣmis
sixth	سادس	sǣdis
seventh	سابع	sǣbi'
eighth	ثامن	tǣmin
ninth	تاسع	tǣsi'
tenth	عاشر	'ǣshir
once	مرة	marra
twice	مرتين	marritēn
three times	ثلاث مرات	tælæt marrāt
a half	نصف	noss
a quarter	ربع	rob'
one third	ثلث	tilt
a pair of	زوج من ...	zōg min
a dozen	دستة [دوزينة]	dæstæ [dozzīnæ]

Time

الثانية عشرة والربع
(itnāshar wæ rob′)

الواحدة و ثلث
(wæḥdæ wæ tilt)

الثانية ونصف الا خمسة
(itnēn wæ noss illæ khæmsæ)

الثالثة والنصف
(tælǣtæ wæ noss)

الرابعة ونصف وخمسة
(arbaa wæ noss wæ khæmsæ)

السادسة الا ثلث
(sittæ illæ tilt)

السابعة الا الربع
(sæb′æ illæ rob′)

الثامنة الا عشرة
(tæmæniæ illæ ashara)

التاسعة الا خمسة
(tisaa illæ khæmsæ)

العاشرة
(ashara)

الحادية عشرة وخمسة
(ḥidāshar wæ khæmsæ)

الثانية عشرة وعشر دقائق
(itnāshar wæ ashara)

Have you got the time?

What time is it?	الساعة كم ؟	ælsææ kææm
It's...	الساعة ...	ælsææ
Excuse me. Can you tell me the time?	الساعة كم من فضلك ؟	ælsææ kææm min **fad**lak
I'll meet you tomorrow...	سأقابلك غداً ...	sæ'okā**bi**lokæ **g**ædæn
at 8 o'clock	الساعة الثامنة	ælsææ tæ**mæn**yæ
at 2.30	الساعة الثانية و النصف	ælsææ 'it**nēn** wæ nisf
Can I come...?	هل يمكننى الحضور ... ؟	hæl yom**ki**noni ælḥo**dūr**
I'm sorry I'm late.	آسف على التأخير .	**'ææ**sif 'ælæl tæ'**khīr**
At what time does... open/close?	متى يفتح / يقفل ... ؟	**mætææ yæf**tæḥ/**yak**fil
What time will it begin/end?	متى يبدأ / ينتهى ؟	**mætææ yæb**dæ'/yæn**tæ**hi
At what time should I be there?	متى يجب أن أصل ؟	**mætææ yæ**gib æn 'asil
At what time will you be there?	متى ستصل ؟	**mætææ** sæ**ta**sil
after/afterwards	بعد / فيما بعد	**bææd**/**fī**mææ **bææd**
before/beforehand	قبل / فيما قبل	kabl/**fī**mææ kabl
early	مبكراً	mobæk**ki**ran
in time	فى الموعد	fil **mæw'**id
late	متأخراً	motæ'ækh**khi**ran
midnight	منتصف الليل	mon**ta**saf æl**lēl**
noon	الساعة الثانية عشر ظهراً	æl **sææ**æ 'it**nā**shar **zoh**ran
hour	ساعة	**sææ**æ
minute	دقيقة	da**kī**ka
second	ثانية [تكة]	**sææ**nyæ [**tæk**kæ]
quarter of an hour	ربع ساعة	rob' **sææ**æ
half an hour	نصف ساعة	nisf **sææ**æ

REFERENCE SECTION

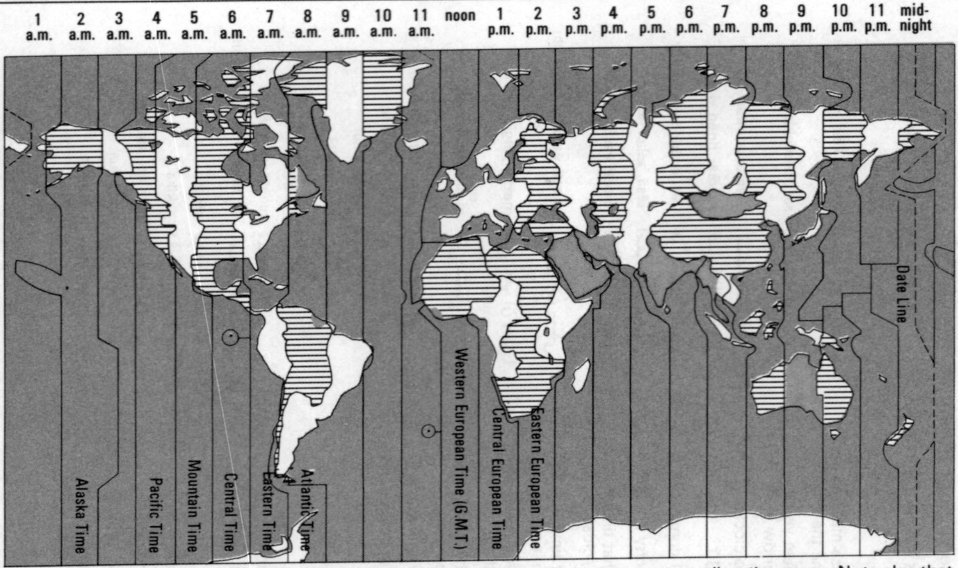

Countries which have adopted a time differing from that in the corresponding time zone. Note also that in the USSR, official time is one hour ahead of the time in each corresponding time zone. In summer, numerous countries advance time one hour ahead of standard time.

Days

What day is it today?	أى الايام اليوم ؟	'æyyil 'ayy**ǣm** æl yōm
Monday	الاثنين	æl 'it**nēn**
Tuesday	الثلاثاء	æl tæ**lǣt**
Wednesday	الاربعاء	æl **'arba'**
Thursday	الخميس	æl khæ**mīs**
Friday	الجمعة	æl **gom**'æ
Saturday	السبت	æl sæbt
Sunday	الاحد	æl 'æḥæd
in the morning	فى الصباح	fil sa**bāḥ**
during the day	خلال اليوم	khi**lǣl** æl yōm
in the afternoon	بعد الظهر	bæædil dohr
in the evening	فى المساء	fil mæ**sǣ**'
at night	فى الليل	fil lēl
yesterday	أمس	'æms
today	اليوم	æl yōm
tomorrow	غداً	gædæn
two days ago	منذ يومين	min yo**mēn**
in three days' time	بعد ثلاثة أيام	bææd tælæt 'æyy**ǣm**
last week	الاسبوع الماضى	æl 'os**bū**' æl **mā**di
next week	الاسبوع القادم	æl 'os**bū**' æl **kā**dim
birthday	عيد ميلاد	'īd mī**lǣd**
day	يوم	yōm
day off	يوم أجازة [فرصة]	yōm 'æ**gǣ**zæ [**fir**sa]
holidays	الاجازة [الفرصة]	æl 'æ**gǣ**zæ [æl **fir**sa]
month	شهر	shahr
vacation	أجازة [فرصة]	'æ**gǣ**zæ [**fir**sa]
week	أسبوع	'os**bū**'
weekday	يوم فى وسط الاسبوع	yōm fī **wis**til 'os**bū**'
weekend	عطلة آخر الاسبوع	'**ot**lit '**ǣ**khir æl 'os**bū**'
working day	يوم عمل	yōm 'æmæl

Months

January	يناير [كانون الثانى]	yænæyir [kænūn æltæni]
February	فبراير [شباط]	fibrāyir [shbāt]
March	مارس [آذار]	mæris [ʹāzār]
April	أبريل [نيسان]	æbrīl [nisæn]
May	مايو [آيار]	mæyo [ʹāyār]
June	يونيو [حزيران]	yonyo [ḥozæyrān]
July	يوليو [تموز]	yolyo [tæmmūz]
August	أغسطس [آب]	ʹagostos [ʹæb]
September	سبتمبر [أيلول]	sibtæmbir [ʹæylūl]
October	اكتوبر [تشرين الاول]	oktōbar [tishrīn æl ʹæwwæl]
November	نوفمبر [تشرين الثانى]	nōvæmbir [tishrīn æl tæni]
December	ديسمبر [كانون الاول]	disæmbir [kænūn æl ʹæwwæl]
since June	منذ شهر يونيو [حزيران]	monzo shahr yonyo [ḥozæyrān]
during the month of August	خلال شهر أغسطس [آب]	khilæl shahr ʹagostos [ʹæb]
last month	الشهر الماضى	æl shahr æl mādi
next month	الشهر القادم	æl shahr æl kādim
July 1	أول يوليو	ʹæwwæl yolyo [tæmmūz]
March 17	السابع عشر من مارس [آذار]	æl sæbii ʹashar min mæris [ʹāzār]

Seasons

spring	الربيع	æl rabīi
summer	الصيف	æl sēf
autumn	الخريف	æl khærīf
winter	الشتاء	æl shitæʹ
in spring	فى الربيع	fil rabīi
during the summer	خلال الصيف	khilæl æl sēf
in autumn	فى الخريف	fil kærīf
during the winter	خلال الشتاء	khilæl æl shitæʹ

Public holidays

Two kinds of calendars are in use in Arab countries. The Gregorian calendar—which is the one we use—is current in normal daily activities. However, newspapers, official documents and certain public holidays follow the Islamic lunar calendar which begins with the Hegira, or emigration of the Prophet Mohammed from Mecca to Medina. 1980 A.D. is the year 1400 of this calendar. The lunar year has twelve months of 29 or 30 days, and thus is approximately 10 days shorter than the Gregorian or solar year.

The names of the Hegira months are:

محرم	moḥarram
صفر	safar
ربيع الاول	rabii æl 'æwwæl
ربيع الثانى	rabii æl tǣni
جمادى الاولى	gæmǣdæ æl 'ūlǣ
جمادى الثانية	gæmǣdæ æl tænyæ
رجب	rægæb
شعبان	shææbǣn
رمضان	ramadān
شوال	shæwwǣl
ذو القعدة	zul kiida
ذو الحجة	zul ḥiggæ

Given below are the most important Moslem holidays.

1st moḥarram	Hegira or Muslim New Year's Day
12th rabii æl 'æwwæl	Birth of the Prophet Mohammed
1st to 3th shæwwæl	Ramadan Baïram ('id æl fitr) celebrating the end of the holy month of Ramadan which is marked by month-long fasting from sunrise to sunset.
9th to 13th zul ḥiggæ	Kurban Baïram ('id æl 'adha) celebrating God's mercy toward Abraham in sparing his son; this is the period during which Muslims make a pilgrimage to Mecca.

While there may be additional regional holidays, only national holidays in Egypt (E), Jordan (J) or Lebanon (L) are cited below:

		E	J	L
January 1	New Year's Day (Gregorian)		J	L
February 9	Saint Maron			L
March 8	March 8th Revolution	E		
March 22	Founding of the Arab League		J	
May 1	Labour Day	E	J	L
May 6	Martyr's Day			L
May 25	Independence Day		J	
June 18	Evacuation Day	E		
July 23	Revolution Anniversary	E		
August 11	Accession Day (King Hussein)		J	
August 15	Assumption Day			L
September 1	September Revolution Day	E		
October 6	October War Day	E		
October 24	Suez Day	E		
November 14	King Hussein's Birthday		J	
November 22	Independence Day			L
December 23	Victoria Day	E		
December 25	Christmas Day		J	L
Movable dates:	Good Friday (Catholic or Orthodox)		J	L
	Easter Monday (Catholic or Orthodox)		J	L
	Spring Day, first Monday after Easter	E		

The year-round temperatures

	Amman	Cairo	Beirut
January	39–54 °F	47–65 °F	51–62 °F
February	40–56	48–69	51–63
March	43–60	52–75	54–66
April	49–73	51–83	58–72
May	57–83	63–91	64–78
June	61–87	68–95	69–83
July	65–89	70–96	73–87
August	65–90	71–95	74–89
September	62–88	68–90	73–86
October	57–81	65–86	69–81
November	50–70	58–78	61–73
December	42–59	50–68	55–65

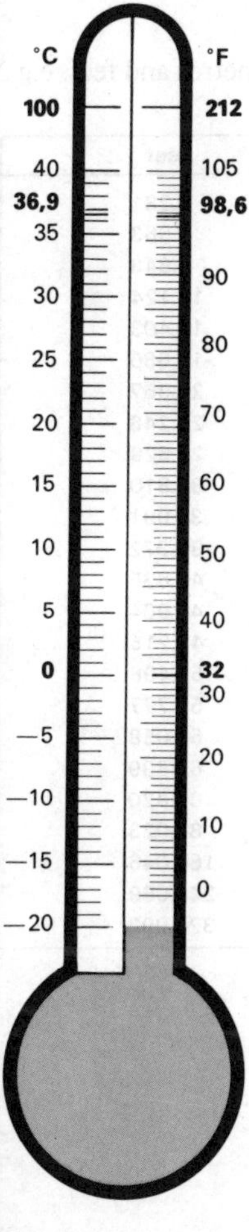

Conversion tables

To change centimetres into inches, multiply by .39.

To change inches into centimetres, multiply by 2.54.

Centimetres and inches

	in.	feet	yards
1 mm	0.039	0.003	0.001
1 cm	0.39	0.03	0.01
1 dm	3.94	0.32	0.10
1 m	39.40	3.28	1.09

	mm	cm	m
1 in.	25.4	2.54	0.025
1 ft.	304.8	30.48	0.305
1 yd.	914.4	91.44	0.914

(32 metres = 35 yards)

Temperature

To convert Centigrade into degrees Fahrenheit, multiply Centigrade by 1.8 and add 32.

To convert degrees Fahrenheit into Centigrade, subtract 32 from Fahrenheit and divide by 1.8.

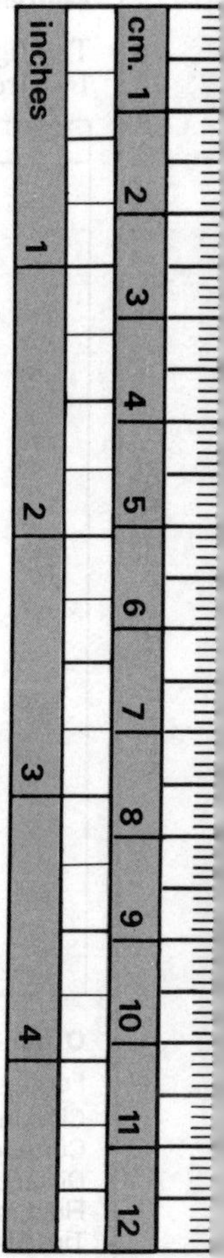

Metres and feet

The figure in the middle stands for both metres and feet, e.g., 1 metre = 3.281 ft. and 1 foot = 0.30 m.

Metres		Feet
0.30	1	3.281
0.61	2	6.563
0.91	3	9.843
1.22	4	13.124
1.52	5	16.403
1.83	6	19.686
2.13	7	22.967
2.44	8	26.248
2.74	9	29.529
3.05	10	32.810
3.35	11	36.091
3.66	12	39.372
3.96	13	42.635
4.27	14	45.934
4.57	15	49.215
4.88	16	52.496
5.18	17	55.777
5.49	18	59.058
5.79	19	62.339
6.10	20	65.620
7.62	25	82.023
15.24	50	164.046
22.86	75	246.069
30.48	100	328.092

Other conversion charts

For see page
Clothing sizes 115
Currency converter 136
Distance (miles-kilometres) 144
Fluid measures 142
Tire pressure 143

Weight conversion

The figure in the middle stands for both kilograms and pounds, e.g., 1 kilogram = 2.205 1b. and 1 pound = 0.45 kilograms.

Kilograms (kg.)		Avoirdupois pounds
0.45	1	2.205
0.91	2	4.409
1.36	3	6.614
1.81	4	8.818
2.27	5	11.023
2.72	6	13.227
3.17	7	15.432
3.62	8	17.636
4.08	9	19.841
4.53	10	22.045
6.80	15	33.068
9.06	20	44.089
11.33	25	55.113
22.65	50	110.225
34.02	75	165.338
45.30	100	220.450

What does that sign mean?

احترس	Caution
احترس من الكلب	Beware of the dog
ادفع	Push
استعلامات	Information
اسحب	Pull
خاص	Private
خالى [فاضى]	Vacant
خروج	Exit
الخزينة	Cashier
خطر	Danger
خطر الموت	Mortal danger
دخول	Entrance
الدخول مجانا	Free entrance
دق الجرس من فضلك	Please ring
رجال	Gentlemen
سيدات	Ladies
طريق خاص	Private road
للايجار	For hire (rent)
للبيع	For sale
مباع	Sold out
مشغول	Occupied
مصعد	Lift (Elevator)
مغلق	Closed
... ممنوع	...forbidden
ممنوع التصوير	No photographs
ممنوع التدخين	No smoking
ممنوع الدخول	No entrance
ممنوع اللمس	Don't touch
ممنوع المرور	No trespassing
منطقة عسكرية	Military area

Emergency!

By the time the emergency is upon you, it's too late to turn to this page to find the Arabic for "Stop thief". So have a look at this list beforehand—and, if you want to be on the safe side, learn the expressions shown in capitals.

Call the police	اطلب البوليس	'otlob æl bolīs
CAREFUL	انتبه	'intæbih
Come here	تعالى هنا	tæǣlæ honǣ
Come in	ادخل	'odkhol
Danger	خطر	khatar
Fire	حريق	ḥærik
Gas	غاز	gǣz
Get a doctor	اطلب دكتور	'otlob doktōr
Get help quickly	اطلب المساعدة بسرعة	'otlob ælmosǣ'ædæ bisoraa
Go away	انصرف	'insarif
HELP	النجدة	ælnægdæ
I'm ill	أنا مريض	ænǣ marīd
I'm lost	أنا تهت	ænǣ toht
Keep your hands to yourself	ابعد يدك	'ibiid yædæk
Leave me alone	اتركنى لحالى	'itrokni liḥǣli
Lie down	ارقد	'orkod
Listen	استمع	istæmii
Look	انظر	onzor
LOOK OUT	احترس	iḥtæris
POLICE	بوليس [شرطة]	bōlīs [shorta]
Quick	بسرعة	bisoraa
STOP	قف	kiff
Stop here	قف هنا	kiff honǣ
Stop that man	امسك هذا الرجل	'æmsik hǣzæ æl ragol
STOP THIEF	امسك حرامى	'æmsik ḥarāmi

FOR CAR ACCIDENTS, see page 149

Index

Quick reference page

Please/Excuse me.	من فضلك .	min **fad**lak
Thank you.	شكراً .	**shok**ran
Yes/No.	أيوة / لا .	'æywæ/lǣ
I beg your pardon/I'm sorry.	آسف .	'**ǣ**sif
Waiter, please.	من فضلك .	min **fad**lak
How much is that?	بكم هذا ؟	bikæm **hǣ**zæ
Where are the toilets?	أين التواليت ؟	'æynæl twæ**lit**

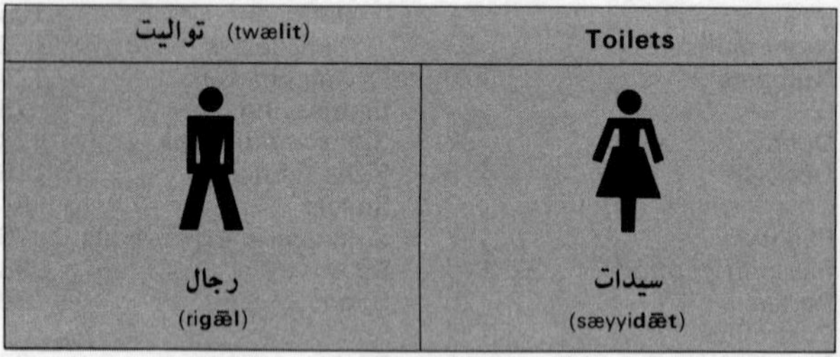

Help me, please.	ساعدنى من فضلك .	sæ'idni min **fad**lak
What time is it?	الساعة كم ؟	ælsǣæ kǣm
Where's the ... consulate?	اين القنصلية ...	'æynæ sel konsoliyyæ
American	الامريكية	sel'æmri**kiy**yæ
English	الانجليزية	sel'ingili**siy**yæ
What does this mean?	ما معنى هذا ؟	mǣ **mæ**ænæ **hǣ**zæ
I don't understand.	لا أفهم .	lǣ '**æf**hæm
Just a minute. I'll point out the word.	لحظة . سأشير الى الكلمة .	**laḥ**za. sæ'o**shīr** 'ilæl·**kil**mæ
Do you speak English?	هل تتكلم انجليزى ؟	hæl tætæ**kæl**læm ingi**lizi**

FRANCE	Brittany French Riviera Loire Valley Paris
GERMANY	Berlin Munich The Rhine Valley
AUSTRIA and SWITZERLAND	Tyrol Vienna Geneva/French-speaking areas Zurich/German-speaking areas Switzerland (192 pages)
GREECE, CYPRUS & TURKEY	Athens Corfu Crete Rhodes Greek Islands of the Aegean Peloponnese Salonica and Northern Greece Cyprus Istanbul*
ITALY and MALTA	Florence Italian Adriatic Italian Riviera Rome Sicily Venice Malta
NETHERLANDS and SCANDINAVIA	Amsterdam Copenhagen Helsinki Oslo and Bergen Stockholm
PORTUGAL	Algarve Lisbon Madeira

*in preparation

SPAIN	Barcelona and Costa Dorada Canary Islands Costa Blanca Costa Brava Costa del Sol and Andalusia Ibiza and Formentera Madrid Majorca and Minorca
EASTERN EUROPE	Budapest Dubrovnik and Southern Dalmatia Hungary (192 pages) Istria and Croatian Coast Moscow & Leningrad Split and Dalmatia
NORTH AMERICA	U.S.A. (256 pages) California Florida Hawaii New York Toronto* Montreal
CARIBBEAN, LATIN AMERICA	Puerto Rico Virgin Islands Bahamas Bermuda French West Indies Jamaica Southern Caribbean Mexico City Rio de Janeiro Caribbean Cruise Guide (368 pages)
EUROPE	Business Travel Guide – Europe (368 pages) Pocket guide to Europe* (384 pages)

Most titles with British and U.S. destinations are available in French, German, Spanish and as many as 7 other languages.

DICTIONARIES

Bilingual with 12,500 concepts each way. Highly practical for travellers, with pronunciation shown plus menu reader, basic expressions and useful information. Over 330 pages.

Danish	Italian
Dutch	Norwegian
Finnish	Portuguese
French	Spanish
German	Swedish

Berlitz Books, a world of information in your pocket! At all leading bookshops and airport newsstands.

Treat yourself to an hour with Berlitz
Just listen and repeat

It's fun, not work. And you'll surprise your friends and yourself with the speed you pick up some basic expressions in the foreign language of your choice. These cassettes are recorded in hi-fi with four voices. Bringing native speakers into your home, they permit you to polish your accent and learn the basic phrases before you depart.

With each cassette is helpful 32-page script, containing pronunciation tips and the complete text of the dual-language recording.

An ideal companion for your Berlitz phrase book, pocket dictionary or travel guide. Order now!

BERLITZ SINGLE CASSETTES
Only $9.95/£5.95 (incl. VAT)

☐ 278 Arabic	☐ 223 Italian
☐ 221 Chinese	☐ 285 Japanese
☐ 297 Danish	☐ 287 Norwegian
☐ 295 Dutch	☐ 279 Portuguese
☐ 296 Finnish	☐ 288 Russian
☐ 219 French	☐ 298 Serbo-Croatian
☐ 220 German	☐ 222 Spanish (Castil.)
☐ 294 Greek	☐ 259 Spanish (Lat. Am.)
☐ 289 Hebrew	☐ 286 Swedish
☐ 299 Hungarian	

TOTAL SINGLES ☐

Please note the total number of each item requested and complete the reverse side of this order form. **11407**

$ From New York	£ From London
Total units ______	Total units ______
at $9.95 each	at £5.95
Total amount enclosed	Total amount enclosed
$ ______	£ ______
(N.Y. residents add sales tax)	(VAT is included)

Name ______________________________

____

Address ____________________________

____

____

Please complete and return this order form to:

Berlitz Publications, Inc.
P.O. Box 506
Delran, N.J. 08370-0506
U.S.A.

or

Cassell Ltd.
1 St. Anne's Road
Eastbourne
East Sussex, BN21 3UN
U.K.

Please order Berlitz books through your bookseller. Should you encounter any difficulties, write directly to any of the distributors listed on the back cover.

11407